California

Real Estate
EXAM
PREP

The SMART Guide to Passing 2e

Thomas Felde

OnCourse Learning

Get licensed. Get ahead.

OnCourse Learning
Get licensed. Get ahead.

California Real Estate Exam Prep: The SMART Guide to Passing 2e

Thomas Felde

Executive Editor: Sara Glassmeyer

Manufacturing Planner: Charlene Taylor

Senior Content Project Manager: Kim Kusnerak

Production Service: S4Carlisle Publishing Services (P) Ltd

Cover Designer: Pop Design Works, www.popdesignworks.com

Cover Images: © ThinkStock Images

Rights Acquisition Director: Audrey Pettengill

Rights Acquisition Specialist, Text and Image: Amber Hosea

For product information and technology assistance, contact us at **Customer & Sales Support, 1-800-354-9706**

Library of Congress Control Number: 2012950902
ISBN-13: 978-1-285-41860-5
ISBN-10: 1-285-41860-3

OnCourse Learning
5191 Natorp Boulevard
Mason, OH 45040
USA

Printed in the United States of America
1 2 3 4 5 6 7 16 15 14 13 12

Introduction

Additional exposure to the material and repetition will improve your confidence and help alleviate "exam anxiety." It is best to answer 100 questions in one sitting. Do not try to answer all of the questions in this book at one time. Take each test as a test. Don't just read a question and then look up the answer. The Sales Exam consists of 150 questions, and you are allowed 3 hours and 15 minutes to complete the exam. Your goal should be to complete about 50 questions per hour.

The Broker Exam is split into two sessions. Each session consists of 100 questions, and you are allowed 2 1/2 hours to complete the session. This means you are allowed 1 1/2 minutes per question.

General Study Hints

Use questions in your book more than once. Write your answers on a separate sheet of paper. This will make scoring easier as you compare your answers with the answer key in the back of the booklet, and leave the questions unmarked for additional "practice" retakes. This will also work with your regular textbook and any other practice exams you might decide to use.

Practice taking timed tests. Duplicate the testing situation by practicing the questions under pressure. This is one of the best ways to overcome exam anxiety. Based on the time allowed on the salespersons state examination, your goal should be to complete 50 questions per hour. For anyone taking the broker's exam, your goal should be to complete each question on average in 1 1/2 minutes. Math questions are going to take more time. Missed items quickly pinpoint your weak areas and help focus your attention on them for additional study.

Research wrong answers. First, carefully read the explanation in the answer key. Determine why the correct answer is correct and the other "distracters" are not. Try not to memorize individual questions, as this may cause you to miss subtle wording differences on the exam, thereby causing you to answer incorrectly. You need to concentrate on concepts, not exact phrasing.

Pace your studying. Immediately test yourself after class discussion. Look up wrong answers. Remember that last-minute cramming before a final exam or the state licensing exam may cause you to panic when confronted with difficult material or to become overly tired during the exam. Do not get behind in your studying; it is difficult to catch up.

Limit your study time. Most people more easily recall the first and last part of whatever they study, while the middle material becomes a little muddled. It is better to study for 10 to 20 minutes with breaks rather than for a solid hour.

Get a good night's sleep before the test. A proper amount of sleep will help you think more clearly and avoid errors from just being tired. "Pulling an all nighter" will just make you tired and often more confused.

Know where you are going. If you are going to a test site in another town, know how to get there and give yourself lots of extra time. Do not add to your frustration by being late!

Know the testing rules. Review your examination guide to be sure you know how you will be tested and the general process. There are generally a few sample questions in the guide, as well as a list of content to be tested. Some of the testing locations are administering the exam on the computer. Don't be too alarmed over the computerized testing procedures, as the procedures are fully explained, and you will be given an opportunity to answer a few sample questions.

Last-minute study. Your last-minute study should include a thorough review of definitions from your regular text. Many of the answers to the questions are merely definitions of various real estate terms. If you struggle with a given topic, don't waste time trying to master it at the very end. Move on and review the material with which you are more familiar.

If you are just beginning a class, try these additional tips:

1. Read the assigned material BEFORE class. If you are in a classroom setting, then the lecture should help reinforce what you have read. Highlight what you think are important points and jot down any questions you might need to ask. Don't highlight everything in your book! Hold your questions until the topic is completed as your question may be answered during the lecture. If ever unsure about asking, speak with the instructor during a break.
2. Participate, don't just talk. Instructors enjoy well-asked questions that give them an opportunity to "teach." However, no one enjoys a classroom where students are continually talking to each other or telling "war stories" that have little to do with the topic.
3. Organize your notes and handouts. Many students accumulate a lot of paper during a class, and it quickly becomes unorganized. Consider using a 3-ring binder or a folder with pockets to stay organized.
4. If you are in a live class, be on time and always listen for instructions. Being late a time or two or daydreaming during class may mean missing a question or two. Those missed items could make the difference between passing and failing.

Test Taking Strategies

- It is always best to schedule your state exam as soon as possible after completing your pre-licensing courses because the information is still fresh in your mind. If you have to delay taking the exam, you may want to join a study group or, better yet, attend a weekend review session.

- The California salesperson's exam consists of 150 questions with a passing grade of 70%. The broker exam consists of a 100-question exam in the morning and a 100-question exam in the afternoon. The passing grade for the 200 questions is 75%. The exams cover 7 major areas of real estate subject matter. 1. Property Ownership and Land Use Controls and Regulations; 2. Laws of Agency; 3. Valuation and Market Analysis; 4. Financing; 5. Transfer of Property; 6. Practice of Real Estate and Mandated Disclosures; 7. Contracts.

- The maximum time you will be allotted for the salesperson examination is a single session of 3 hours and 15 minutes. The maximum time you will be allotted for the broker examination is five hours, administered in one 2 1/2-hour morning session and one 2 1/2-hour afternoon session.

- Less than ten percent of the questions on both the salesperson and broker exams are math-related. It is logical for those of you who consider yourselves to be "mathematically challenged" to concentrate your study efforts on law and practice. You can answer all the math problems incorrectly and still pass the exam if you have mastered the other areas. Keep in mind that you are allowed to use a calculator during the exam. If math seems to be one of your weak points, skip all of the math questions until the end of the exam. As a last resort, make a guess. Never leave the answer to any question blank.

- Many exam takers accuse the State of using "trick questions" on the exam. This is not true. Many times a question appears to have two correct answers. There is only one correct answer, so read the two choices carefully and try to choose the correct answer based on your knowledge of the subject matter. Occasionally, you will find a question that reads "all of the following are correct except." In this case, you are looking for an incorrect statement, not any of the three correct statements.

- Regarding proration questions, you can usually eliminate two out of the four answer choices without even doing the calculations. You just have to remember that in prorations, the amounts credited to one party are the same as those credited to the other. If the answer choice states that "the seller is debited **$142.98**," and the buyer is credited with **$56.02**, "it is **NOT** the correct answer. If the answer states that "the seller is debited **$142.98** and the buyer is credited **$142.98**," it **MAY** be the correct choice since the figures are the same.

- There are a number of items that you will be prohibited from bringing into the examination room on the day of your examination. These prohibited items include: backpacks, briefcases, suitcases, food, drink, study materials, portable computers, PDAs (personal digital assistants), or programmable calculators. In addition, you will be prohibited from using your cell phone during the examination. Once you enter the examination room, your cell phone must be turned off and placed out of your sight.

- You will be permitted to use the following items during your examination: a silent, battery-operated, electronic, pocket-size calculator that does *not* have a print capability or an alphabetic keyboard. Cell phone calculators are not permitted.

- If you haven't done so already, check the California Department of Real Estate website for the most current information on the California real estate licensing examinations: http://www.dre.ca.gov

State Exam Outline

	Approximate Percentage of Questions on the Exam	
	Salesperson	Broker
Property Ownership and Land Use Controls and Regulations	15%	15%
Laws of Agency and Fiduciary Duties	17%	17%
Property Valuation and Financial Analysis	14%	14%
Financing	9%	9%
Transfer of Property	8%	8%
Practice of Real Estate and Mandated Disclosures	25%	25%
Contracts	12%	12%
	100%	100%

Expanded State Exam Outline

The following expanded outlines are provided to give you a general idea of the topics that may appear on the California salesperson and broker examinations. These outlines are not intended to be a comprehensive list of topics that will appear on the examinations.

1. Property Ownership and Land Use Controls and Regulations

   ☑ Classes of property
   ☑ Property characteristics
   ☑ Encumbrances
   ☑ Types of ownership
   ☑ Descriptions of property
   ☑ Government rights in land
   ☑ Public controls
   ☑ Environmental hazards and regulations
   ☑ Private controls
   ☑ Water rights
   ☑ Special categories of land

2. Laws of Agency and Fiduciary Duties

   ☑ Law, definition and nature of agency relationships, types of agencies, and agents
   ☑ Creation of agency and agency agreements
   ☑ Responsibilities of agent to seller/buyer as principal
   ☑ Disclosure of agency
   ☑ Disclosure of acting as principal or other interest
   ☑ Termination of agency
   ☑ Commission and fees
   ☑ Responsibilities of agent to non-client third parties

3. Property Valuation and Financial Analysis

   ☑ Value
   ☑ Methods of estimating value
   ☑ Financial analysis

4. Financing

   ☑ General Concepts
   ☑ Types of loans
   ☑ Sources of financing
   ☑ Government programs
   ☑ Mortgages/deeds of trust/notes
   ☑ Financing/credit laws
   ☑ Loan brokerage
   ☑ Types of loan originators

5. Transfer of Property

- ☑ Title Insurance
- ☑ Deeds
- ☑ Escrow
- ☑ Tax aspects
- ☑ Special processes
- ☑ Transfer through court supervision
- ☑ Types of vesting

6. Practice of Real Estate and Mandated Disclosures

- ☑ Trust account management
- ☑ Fair housing laws
- ☑ Truth in advertising
- ☑ Record keeping requirements
- ☑ Agency supervision
- ☑ Permitted activities of unlicensed sales assistants
- ☑ Department of Real Estate (DRE) jurisdiction and disciplinary actions
- ☑ Licensing, continuing education requirements and procedures
- ☑ California Real Estate Recovery Fund
- ☑ General ethics
- ☑ Technology
- ☑ Property management
- ☑ Commercial/industrial/income properties
- ☑ Specialty areas
- ☑ Transfer disclosure statement
- ☑ Natural hazard disclosure statements
- ☑ Disclosure of material facts affecting property value
- ☑ Need for inspection and obtaining/verifying information
- ☑ Reports
- ☑ Servicing diverse populations

7. Contracts

- ☑ General
- ☑ Listing agreements
- ☑ Buyer broker agreements
- ☑ Offers/purchase contracts
- ☑ Agreements
- ☑ Promissory notes/securities
- ☑ Purchase/lease options
- ☑ Advanced fee

1. A lease for a three-year term that called for rent to be paid quarterly expired. If at the end of the term, the landlord were to accept another payment of rent, the lease would be

A. extended another three years.
B. a periodic tenancy.
C. extended for a term not to exceed one year.
D. cancelled in any event.

2. Marx gets to one of his barns by driving across McDonald's land. He has been making the drive daily for the past six years. McDonald had often asked Marx to stop this practice. Marx now says he has a legal right to continue this use of McDonald's land. Marx's right, if valid, is an easement by

A. necessity.
B. implied grant.
C. prescription.
D. defeasance.

3. The general term value means

A. the function of an object.
B. the average use and function of an object to all people.
C. the worth, usefulness, or utility of an object to someone for some purpose.
D. a good buy.

4. A prospective purchaser obtained a four-month option on a parcel of real property by paying $200 to the owner. All of the following are true EXCEPT

A. the optionee has created a legal interest in the property.

B. the optionor is totally restricted by having received a "valuable" consideration.
C. the agreement imposes no obligation on the optionee to purchase the property.
D. a unilateral contract has been created.

5. Race restrictions limiting the sale or lease of property to persons of the Caucasian race were imposed on a subdivision in 1920, due to expire in 2020. The restrictions are presently

A. valid, as long as the original owner is still alive.
B. unenforceable, even if the majority of homeowners want them.
C. enforceable, if the buyer agrees.
D. binding.

6. All of the following would have an effect on the final estimate of value when making an appraisal of an old family residence except:

A. Purpose of the appraisal.
B. Suitability of the residence to the site.
C. Physical condition of the building.
D. Original cost of the building.

7. How long does a victim have to file a complaint about discrimination with the Department of Housing and Urban Development?

A. Three months
B. Six months
C. Nine months
D. One year

8. The best synonym for "value" is

A. cost.
B. worth.
C. uselessness.
D. asking price.

9. In real estate "devise" refers to

A. a conveyance or real property by will.
B. an inheritance.
C. destruction of man-made structures by acts of god.
D. probate action when one dies intestate.

10. Under federal income tax law, the basis of real property is the property's

A. purchase price minus any existing assumed loans.
B. assessed value prior to sale.
C. fair market value.
D. original cost plus cost of any improvements.

11. If you hold an undivided interest in the common areas, and a separate interest in a specific unit of an industrial, commercial or residential building, you would own a

A. stock cooperative.
B. condominium unit.
C. community apartment project.
D. land project.

12. A listing agreement is essentially a/an

A. employment contract.
B. purchase contract.
C. option to sell.
D. all of the above.

13. Which of the following is an "interest" but not an "estate" in real property?

A. Remainder
B. Mortgage
C. Reversion
D. Leasehold

14. Which of the following is correct concerning delinquent taxes and redemption rights?

A. The important effect of a "sale to the state" by the tax collector is to start the redemption period running, but the delinquent owner's possession remains undisturbed.
B. The homeowner is required to make monthly installment payments to liquidate the delinquent property taxes and accrued penalties that are owed.
C. In the event the delinquent owner transfers or otherwise alienates the property, the redemption period is automatically terminated.
D. The property is automatically deeded to the state if the property is not redeemed within one year.

15. The "Mortgagor" is the one who

A. sells the property.
B. signs the note.
C. holds the trust.
D. accepts a mortgage.

16. The majority of money used for loans on real estate comes from

A. individual savings.
B. federal reserves.
C. co-op savings.
D. government bonds.

17. Which of the following is required for a valid escrow in the conveyance of title to real property?

A. The services of a licensed real estate broker.
B. A binding contract between buyer and seller and the conditional delivery of transfer instruments to a third party.
C. A complete chain of title.
D. No conditions in the escrow instructions.

18. A testament is a

A. will.
B. sandwich lease.
C. pledge.
D. negotiable instrument.

19. Definitions of market value are least concerned with

A. material cost.
B. value in exchange.
C. objective value.
D. an open market.

20. The key factor in a developer's decision in choosing the best site to build a new shopping center in a suburban area would be

A. purchasing power.
B. topography.
C. traffic count.
D. population.

21. A voidable contract is one that

A. is valid now but can be voided by an interested party for due cause.
B. is binding on neither party and not subject to ratification.
C. has no force or effect.
D. is subject to disciplinary action.

22. Which of the following would not be true in the planning and development of a subdivision?

A. Minor streets entering major streets at right angles are proper.
B. Short blocks are economical.
C. Excessively deep lots are wasteful.
D. Sharply angled lots create engineering problems.

23. Putting together two or more parcels to form a large parcel under one ownership is called

A. aggregating.
B. compounding.
C. turn over.
D. assemblage.

24. A "Trust Deed" is:

A. the mere incident of the debt.
B. security for the note.
C. terminated after four years of nonpayment on the loan.
D. held by the trustor.

25. When the appraiser is concerned with equilibrium and decline of value in her appraisal, she most likely would apply this to

A. the neighborhood.
B. commercial property.
C. industrial property.
D. agricultural property.

26. Mrs. King borrowed money using a fully amortized loan to finance the remodeling of her real property. If equal monthly payments include both principal and interest, the amount of the payment on the principal will:

A. Increase at a constant amount.
B. Decline while the amount credited to interest increases.
C. Cause the amount credited to interest to remain constant.
D. Increase while the amount credited to interest decreases.

27. An impound account will benefit the

A. beneficiary and the trustor.
B. trustee.
C. trustor only.
D. beneficiary only.

28. An easement in gross

A. benefits dominant tenement.
B. burdens servient tenement.
C. cannot be owned separately from an interest in land.
D. burdens dominant tenement.

29. A straight note

A. may be used in a real estate transaction.
B. is a note providing that the principal owing is to be paid at one time.
C. may be secured by a mortgage.
D. may be any of the above.

30. When a judgment is duly recorded, subsequent buyers and innocent purchasers who are ignorant of the recording have received

A. constructive notice.
B. contingent notice.
C. actual notice.
D. voidable notice.

31. Assume a brother and a sister own title in a parcel of real property as joint tenants. The sister marries and deeds half her interest to her husband. Under these circumstances, the brother now holds title to the property as

A. a joint tenant.
B. community property.
C. sole owner.
D. a tenant in common.

32. The court order to sell property to satisfy a judgment is a

A. Trustee's Sale.
B. Certificate of Sale.
C. Writ of Execution.
D. Writ of Possession.

33. As defined in the California Subdivision Law: a subdivision of fifty or more lots or parcels having certain stated characteristics is referred to as a Land Project. A subdivision of fifty or more parcels is specifically excluded from treatment as a Land Project when

A. lots are not offered for sale by means of substantial direct mail advertising, and sales and promotion costs are nominal.
B. all lots are to be offered for sale to builders or developers only.
C. all parcels in the subdivision are part of a planned unit development.
D. either "A" or "B" above.

34. Title to personal property is transferred by

A. Bill of Sale.
B. Notice of bulk transfer.
C. Chattel mortgage.
D. Security agreement.

35. A rectangular parcel of land has an area of 540 square yards. It has a 45 foot frontage. How deep is the lot?

A. 60 feet
B. 108 feet
C. 1,080 feet
D. 200 yards

36. Mr. Anderson purchased an apartment for $100,000 paying $37,500 down and financing the balance. About two years later he sold the property for $115,000 and realized a 40% increase on his original investment. This would be an example of

A. escalation.
B. leverage.
C. plotting.
D. highest and best use.

37. Buyer Smith agrees to take over the existing fire insurance policy presently in effect on the property in the name of the seller, Mr. Wilson. When will Smith be protected by this policy?

A. Immediately upon notifying the insurer of the name change
B. Upon receiving possession of the property
C. At close of escrow
D. When the insurer approves the assignment

38. A man purchased a personal residence in 2005 for $263,000. In 2006 he remodeled, spending $34,000 for capital improvements. In 2012 he sold his residence for $385,000 and purchased a replacement residence within a few months for $400,000. The amount of taxable gain at this time from the sale of the original residence is

A. $88,000.
B. $122,000.
C. $137,000.
D. Nothing.

39. A real estate broker's license could be revoked or suspended by the Real Estate Commissioner for any of the following reasons EXCEPT

A. he has failed to supervise his salesperson.
B. he has demonstrated negligence or incompetence in performing a real estate act.
C. he has been convicted of fraud in a court suit levied against him for the loss.
D. two reliable witnesses have given sworn testimony that the broker is mentally ill.

40. Under which of the following circumstances would a deed be void?

A. Grantor uses a name that is not his true name.
B. Grantee is a fictitious person.
C. The spelling of the name of the grantor in the body of the deed differs from that in the signature.
D. Grantee is sufficiently described in the deed but he is not named therein.

41. Which of the following items is often short-rated?

A. An interest rate
B. Premiums on an insurance policy
C. Taxes on a single-family residence
D. Maintenance charges on an apartment building

42. A broker's trust fund records must show the trust fund balance on which basis?

A. Daily
B. Weekly (each Friday)
C. Monthly (first of month)
D. Quarterly (first of quarter)

43. An attachment is classified as a/an

A. judgment.
B. lien.
C. encroachment.
D. appurtenance.

44. The only unity required for the existence of a tenancy in common is

A. possession.
B. time.
C. title.
D. interest.

45. The owner of an undivided interest in land with another with no right of survivorship owns the land as

A. a joint tenant.
B. in severalty.
C. absolute ownership.
D. a tenant in common.

46. A buyer purchased a home for $80,000 using a down payment of 21.25% of the purchase price, and financing the balance on a 30-year amortized loan with interest at 10.25% per annum. The lender requires monthly impounds for property taxes of $800 per year and casualty insurance costing $978 for a three-year policy. Assuming that the first monthly payment on the principal is $119, the total amount the buyer will have to pay the first month will be approximately

A. $250.
B. $357.
C. $751.
D. $827.

47. When the Environmental Review Board or the Department of Real Estate issues a "negative declaration," it means that the subdivision

A. has not been approved by the Real Estate Commissioner for the issuance of a public report.
B. public report contains notations of possible adverse environmental impacts.
C. will have an insignificant effect upon the environment.
D. has been approved, subject to compliance with provisions for mitigating adverse environmental conditions.

48. Every non-resident applicant for a California Real Estate license must, along with the application, file with the Real Estate Commissioner a/an

A. statement by the applicant's home state Real Estate Commissioner stating that the applicant is duly licensed by his home state.
B. application fee of 1 1/2 times the California license fee.
C. copy of a statement filed by the applicant's County Recorder showing the applicant is residing in that county and will operate in that county.
D. consent that if any action is commenced against him in California and personal service of process upon him can't be made, a valid service may be made by delivery process to the Secretary of State.

49. The most difficult step in the capitalization approach is to

A. establish the annual net income.
B. establish the annual gross income.
C. find comparable sales.
D. select the appropriate capitalization rate.

50. A turnkey project is a/an

A. residential subdivision that is completed and ready for occupancy.
B. low income housing project subsidized by the government.
C. illegal subdivision.
D. vacant lot with complete architectural plans.

51. The vertical supporting timbers between the floor and ceiling are

A. beams.
B. studs.
C. the ridge board.
D. joists.

52. Broker Bart was taken to court by a client who was suing the broker for fraud in a real estate transaction. The client was successful and was awarded damages in the civil suit. After the judgment has been handed down, the Real Estate Commissioner can immediately

A. revoke the broker's license.
B. suspend the broker's license pending a hearing.
C. file an accusation and statement of issues and proceed against the broker.
D: hold a hearing with his deputies to decide if a Notice of Suspension should be mailed.

53. The purpose of a Deed is to

A. transfer title to real property from one party to another.
B. show the persons involved in the title transfer.
C. create a written document suitable for recording.
D. create a document that, when recorded, will give actual notice of ownership.

54. Rezoning a section of town and changing its lawful use for new development from commercial to residential use is known as

A. redevelopment planning.
B. a variance.
C. a referendum.
D. down zoning.

55. The Franchise Investment Law is written primarily for the protection of

A. franchisees and/or sub-franchisers who have purchased rights to an exclusive geographic territory.
B. stockholders of franchiser corporations with a net worth of less than $500,000.
C. prospective franchisees when considering the purchase of a franchise.
D. none of the above.

56. In a valid Quitclaim Deed

A. the grantor must be seized of fee.
B. the only warranty is the expressed or implied warranty that the grantor owns, or has an interest in, the property.
C. there is a conveyance of after-acquired title.
D. none of the above.

57. Using borrowed funds when available at rates that are below the equity yield of an investment property

A. is illegal.
B. increases the cash flow.
C. enhances the equity yield.
D. decreases the equity yield.

58. A "real estate appraisal" is an estimate of value

A. based upon replacement costs.
B. based upon analysis of facts as of a specific date.
C. derived from income data covering at least the preceding six months.
D. derived from average tax assessments covering the past five years.

59. Freehold estates would include which of the following

A. a life estate.
B. an leasehold estate.
C. an estate for years.
D. all of the above.

60. A real estate salesperson is defined by law as "a natural person who, in expectation of a compensation is employed by a real estate broker to perform any of the acts set forth in the law." In such capacity, however, he/she may not

A. sign for the broker in any listing or deposit receipt.
B. collect his or her commission directly from the owner.
C. agree to work for less than 50% of the earned commission.
D. be paid a commission by his broker for negotiating a loan.

61. A real estate salesperson's relationship with his broker is comparable to that of

A. lessor to lessee.
B. an independent contractor to his or her principal.
C. a sub-agent to his or her agent.
D. an employee to his or her employer.

62. A contract according to the "Statute of Frauds" must be in writing to be enforceable to

A. employ a real estate broker to sell stock, trade fixtures and goodwill of a business.
B. employ a real estate broker to negotiate a lease for a one-year term.
C. employ a real estate broker to exchange one-year leases on properties zoned for retail business.
D. handle any agreement not to be performed within one year.

63. Which of the following would alienate title to property?

A. Recording a homestead
B. Securing an "Alta Title Policy" of title insurance
C. Conveying title
D. Clouding the title

64. When the Real Estate Commissioner desires a formal opinion on legal matters, he consults the

A. County District Attorney.
B. Secretary of State of California.
C. Attorney General of California.
D. California Corporations Commissioner.

65. The answers to which of the following questions would be of most benefit when trying to determine the amount of economic obsolescence suffered by a commercial property?

A. Is the rental schedule of the building equitably charged to the tenants?
B. Can a building be operated efficiently?
C. Are the tenants in the neighborhood prospering?
D. Should a fire escape be installed?

66. A real estate investor who wishes to operate by using the principle of leverage would

A. use his personal funds insofar as possible.
B. use borrowed funds and personal funds on an equal basis.
C. use borrowed money to the maximum extent possible.
D. invest in real properties with values that are declining.

67. The Prepaid Rental Listing Agent is required to do all of the following EXCEPT

A. give a contract and receipt to every prospective tenant, which provides for return of the fee under certain conditions.
B. repay any amount over $25 if a rental is not obtained.
C. return the entire fee if no referrals are received within five days of the execution of the agreement.
D. submit a statement of accounts to the Commissioner quarterly.

68. An attachment lien is valid for:

A. One year
B. Two years
C. Three years
D. Four years

69. In a listing agreement, the property is described as "Mr. Leland's personal residence at 10th and Jackson Streets, in Modesto, California." Which of the following statements is true?

A. The listing is void if this description was used.
B. This description would only be adequate if Mr. Leland owned this one property on that street.

C. This description would be adequate even if Mr. Leland owned other properties on that same street.
D. The title would be uninsurable should the listing contain this description.

70. The seller accepted an offer for the purchase of real property and an escrow was opened. Later the seller discovered misrepresentation on the part of the buyer. The contract

A. is valid as to the seller.
B. may be voided by the seller.
C. is void.
D. is invalid.

71. An appraiser is preparing the income approach to an appraisal of income property. In his selection of a capitalization rate, he must recognize that the higher the rate used, the greater the implied

A. income.
B. appreciation.
C. risk.
D. value.

72. Which item will appear as a debit on the buyer's closing statement?

A. The purchase price
B. Prepaid rents
C. Prepaid property taxes
D. None of the above.

73. In appraising a home, one of the factors that would affect the appraised value is

A. the number of square feet in the structure.
B. the owner's book value or cost basis.
C. the current financing on the property.
D. none of the above.

74. The economic life of an improvement is the period of time that is

A. equal to, or the same as, the improvement's physical life.
B. between the completion of the building and its inability to produce income.
C. beyond the improvement's physical life.
D. over when it stops producing income equal to taxes, maintenance, and utilities.

75. A bank gave $500 to a licensed real estate salesperson for referring the salesperson's prospective buyer to the bank for a new loan. When the salesperson's broker became aware of the $500 referral fee, the broker immediately fired the salesperson, notified the Real Estate Commissioner and warned all of his other salespeople never to accept such a fee. In this situation

A. the bank is subject to disciplinary action by the Real Estate Commissioner.
B. the salesperson is subject to disciplinary action by the Real Estate Commissioner, but the broker is not.
C. the salesperson and broker are subject to disciplinary action by the Real Estate Commissioner.
D. the broker overreacted because a referral fee is legal.

76. Property may be technically defined as

A. less than freehold estates.
B. things owned by buyers and sellers.
C. rights or interests that a person has in the thing owned.
D. fee simple absolute.

77. Mr. Jackson owns a home that is situated at the bottom of a hillside. In the wintertime during heavy rainstorms his home is subject to damage by flooding, so he dug a trench along the back of his property to divert the water. This action would be

A. legal if the water is diverted to a vacant lot.
B. illegal because you cannot divert surface waters to another property to the detriment of the other property.
C. legal because every owner has the right to protect his property against flooding.
D. illegal because he is violating the riparian rights law.

78. The value of real estate is created, maintained and destroyed by the interplay of three great forces. Not included in these three are

A. social ideals and standards.
B. private restrictions.
C. government regulations.
D. economic adjustments.

79. A subdivider is occasionally given a preliminary public report by the Commissioner. Which of the following would invalidate that preliminary public report?

A. A material change in the ownership of the subdivision properties
B. A material change in the size of the lots
C. The expiration of the preliminary public report, or the issuance of the final public report
D. All of the above.

80. If five people own property as joint tenants

A. they need not own equal interest in the property.
B. there is still only one title to the whole property.
C. if one of the owners dies, his heirs become tenants in common with the surviving co-owners.
D. each co-owner has a separate legal title to his undivided interest.

81. "Loan-to-Value Ratio" is

A. monthly payments compared to the original amount due on the promissory note.
B. mortgage loan amount compared to percentage of sales price.
C. mortgage loan amount compared to percentage of assessed value.
D. mortgage loan amount compared to percentage of appraised value.

82. What would be the maximum commission that could be charged on a second deed of trust in the amount of $4,000, for a term of three years?

A. $600
B. $400
C. $200
D. Anything

83. Mr. and Mrs. Walter Layman hold title to their property as joint tenants. Mrs. Layman has had a will drawn in which she, upon her death, transfers her interest in the home to the children equally. Concerning her will upon her death, which of the following would be true?

A. The children have no interest whatsoever in the property.
B. Each child will have a half interest in the property.

C. One-half will go to the children and one-half to the father.
D. The property must be probated to determine correct ownership.

84. The five requisites for a valid land contract are

A. legality, capacity of the parties, mutuality, offer/acceptance, writing.
B. consideration, offer/acceptance, mutuality, capacity of the parties, writing.
C. mutuality, consideration, offer/acceptance, legality, legal object.
D. consideration, offer/acceptance, legality, capacity of the parties, writing.

85. A "Prepayment Penalty Clause" benefits

A. the beneficiary.
B. the trustee.
C. the trustor.
D. all of the above.

86. Concerning value, which of the following is the most important factor?

A. Location
B. Price asked
C. Current use of the property
D. Future anticipated use of the property

87. The California Real Estate Law is a part of the

A. Business and Professions Code.
B. Government Code.
C. Administrative Code.
D. Corporations Code.

88. Which of the following is usually required to report the sale of a single-family residence to the Internal Revenue Service?

A. Broker
B. Buyer
C. Escrow
D. Seller

89. There is a Federal Law that is designed to protect purchasers of subdivision properties that are located in the United States and are being offered for sale in interstate commerce. This law provides for a right of rescission within

A. three days.
B. five days.
C. seven days.
D. ten days.

90. A real estate agent acting under an exclusive agency agreement signed by the seller owes a fiduciary obligation to

A. the buyer.
B. the seller.
C. both the buyer and the seller.
D. primarily to the seller and partially to the buyer.

91. How many township survey coordinate systems are there in California?

A. Two
B. Three
C. Four
D. Five

92. In California, a typical sale of real property involves the transfer of which type of estate?

A. Community property
B. A fee
C. Corporate ownership
D. Stock cooperative

93. Which of the following business opportunity documents would compare most nearly to a deed?

A. Security Agreement
B. Bill of Sale
C. Lease Option
D. Financing Statement

94. A developer can use the Improvement Act of 1911 as amended to raise funds for all of the following purposes, EXCEPT to:

A. purchase land for subdivision.
B. provide for drainage.
C. construct sewers.
D. develop off-site improvements.

95. Broker Knorr advertised in the newspaper that anyone who bought a property listed with the broker would receive a free microwave oven valued at $500. Such action is

A. legal provided full disclosure is made to all interested parties.
B. illegal under any circumstances.
C. legal provided that only a chance to win the microwave in a drawing is actually given to the buyer.
D. illegal since the value of such a gift cannot exceed $100.

96. When John purchased Joan's property using an installment sales contract, he assumed an existing loan, which exceeded Joan's basis in the property. The amount of the assumed loan over Joan's basis will be

A. deducted from Joan's basis.
B. treated as part of the sales price.
C. added to Joan's basis.
D. treated as part of the down payment whether cash was received or not.

97. Tom Davis owns a single-family residence in which he, his wife, and five children reside. In filling out his income tax return he itemizes his various allowable deductions. The following expense would NOT be allowed as a deduction:

A. Real property taxes
B. Interest on the loan
C. Cost of repainting exterior
D. Uninsured casualty losses

98. Which of the following includes the characteristic "of indefinite duration"?

A. Estate from period to period
B. Estate of inheritance
C. Estate for years
D. Less than freehold estate

99. Based on the energy efficiency rating given new air conditioners today, the higher the EER, the

A. more BTU's produced.
B. less efficient the appliance.
C. greater the wattage used by the appliance.
D. higher the efficiency of the appliance.

100. A one-year lease on real property signed by a 16-year-old minor is

A. valid if he is single and has never been married.
B. valid if he is married.
C. invalid if he is married and his wife has not signed the lease.
D. invalid unless approval is given by a court appointed guardian, regardless of his marital status.

101. Which of the following is described as the process of expressing anticipated future benefits of ownership in dollars?

and discounting them to a present worth at a rate which is attracting purchase capital to similar investments?

A. Yield evaluation
B. Capitalization
C. Projection
D. Equity manipulation

102. The person who most likely would make use of the legal remedy known as "Unlawful Detainer" would be a:

A. Trustor
B. Holder of a note in default
C. Lessor
D. Grantor

103. A real estate broker hired a salesperson and entered into a written contract of employment, designating him/her as an Independent Contractor. Such status permits the salesman to

A. advertise listed properties in his own name.
B. sue to collect a commission in his own name.
C. work for several brokers at one time.
D. perform his services only through his employing broker.

104. The maximum amount of income which rental property can be expected to produce is known as:

A. Effective gross income
B. Gross scheduled income
C. Net operating income
D. None of the above.

105. A broker is required to keep his principal informed of all material facts. A broker who holds a listing from the seller must disclose which of the following facts when presenting an offer?

A. The purchaser is not of the Caucasian race
B. A cooperating broker will be presenting a higher offer the following day
C. The buyer's lender is insisting on an impound account
D. None of the above.

106. Broker Newman sold a property owned by Robins to Buyer Nichols. Later when the first rains of the season began, Buyer Nichols found that the roof leaked badly. Thereupon, the buyer sued both the seller and the broker for the cost of the necessary repairs. In the same action, the seller sued Broker Newman because Seller Robins had told the broker of the leaky roof. Broker Newman's testimony revealed that the broker was aware of the leaky rook but had not mentioned it to Buyer Nichols because "the subject never came up." Based on the foregoing information, the most likely result of the court action would be

A. on the basis of the principle of caveat emptor, the buyer was not entitled to recover from either the broker or the seller.
B. the buyer recovered from the broker, but the seller would not be considered liable.
C. the buyer recovered from the seller, but the broker would not be liable.
D. the buyer would be successful in the suit against both the seller and the broker; the seller would be successful in the suit against the broker.

107. Adams sold his house to Brooks, who did not record the deed, but took up residency there. Adams then sold the same property, to Carr, who reviewed the county recorder's records, but did not examine the property. Adams gave Carr a deed, which Carr recorded. Which of the following would be true concerning title to the property?

A. Carr and Brooks are co-owners of the property.
B. Carr now owns the property, because he recorded his deed first.
C. Carr has recourse against Brooks for failure to record.
D. Brooks maintains title.

108. For income tax purposes, on which of the following could depreciation be taken?

A. Raw land
B. Owner occupied residential property
C. Owner occupied farmhouse
D. Peach orchards

109. For an inflation hedge, one would most likely put their money into

A. a savings account.
B. government backed trust deeds or mortgages.
C. long term government bonds.
D. real property.

110. A franchise being offered for sale in the State of California does not need to be registered with the Department of Corporations Commissioner if the franchisor

A. is a firm incorporated in another state.
B. has a net worth on a consolidated basis of $5,000.
C. has a net worth on a consolidated basis of $1,000,000.
D. has a net worth on a consolidated basis of $5,000,000 or more.

111. Certain factors to be considered in evaluating business property are given special names by appraisers. The name given to the factor that affords the advantage of display area and entrances on two streets is called

A. pedestrian count.
B. corner influence.
C. 100% location.
D. accessibility.

112. The principal characteristics of Fee Simple Title include all of the following EXCEPT:

A. it is free of encumbrances.
B. it may be willed.
C. it is transferable.
D. it is of indefinite duration

113. "O," the owner of Blackmore, sold it to "A," but reserved to himself a life estate, and remained in possession. Later, "O" sold his life estate to "B," and surrendered possession to him. "A" then demanded immediate possession as the fee owner. In this situation

A. "A" is entitled to possession.
B. "B" should sue for the return of his purchase price.
C. "O" is liable for damages to "A."
D. "B" can retain possession as long as "O" lives.

114. Jed gives Jake a written option allowing Jake to buy Jed's house for $100,000 within 18 months from the date of the option. Jake gives Jed $ 0.25 payment in exchange for the option. The option is

A. void for lack of sufficient consideration.

B. voidable for lack of consideration, but only at Jed's discretion.
C. valid; the consideration is sufficient.
D. unenforceable because the option right extends beyond one year.

115. Mortgage interest rates usually decrease when

A. the supply of mortgage money increases substantially.
B. inflationary trends are on the upswing.
C. businesses are expanding and making large capital expenditures.
D. the Federal Reserve Board increases the reserve requirements for member banks.

116. Under most circumstances it is unlawful for anyone to act as an escrow holder unless they have been licensed by the Commissioner of the Department of Corporations. Whom of the following would be in violation of the law?

A. The real estate broker who holds an escrow for a buyer and a seller for whom he had represented in the sale.
B. The real estate broker who solicits escrows from his fellow brokers and agrees to make no charge for the work.
C. The attorney at law who handles an escrow for a fee on behalf of his clients.
D. The licensed escrow company that is incorporated and advertises for escrows for a fee.

117. If a seller of real property inquired of his broker concerning the ethnic background of a prospective buyer, the broker

A. Should secure the permission of the buyer's broker before revealing such information.
B. Would be obligated by his fiduciary duty to disclose all material facts and therefore must disclose the requested information.
C. Violates the California Fair Housing Act (the Rumford Act) if he gives the seller the requested information.
D. Could give the seller the requested information as long as it is pointed out that the information may not be used to discriminate against the buyer.

118. Which department, bureau or board of the state of California receives the Structural Pest Control Reports?

A. The Bureau of Entomology
B. The Department of Real Estate
C. The Structural Pest Control Board
D. No bureau. It remains with the city or county where the inspection occurred.

119. Under the Truth-in-Lending Law, which of the following is not to be included in the finance charge?

A. Appraisal fee
B. Loan points
C. Time/price differential
D. Finder's fees and similar charges

120. Concerning the following, which would be correct?

A. A note is the security for a trust deed
B. A trust deed has more value than a note
C. A trust deed is security for a note
D. The note must be recorded to perfect a lien on the property

121. The highest structural point of a wood frame house is the

A. girder.
B. ridge board.
C. collar beam.
D. header.

122. A broker secures a listing, negotiates a sale, and the parties enter escrow. Before escrow closes, the broker's license is revoked and the seller refuses to pay the commission because the broker is unlicensed. To collect the commission, the following is correct?

A. Broker must prove he actually introduced the buyer to the seller.
B. Broker must prove that he was licensed at the time of sale.
C. Broker must prove that he executed the sales contract.
D. Broker cannot sue for a commission in view of license revocation.

123. A contract for the sale of community real property signed by the husband only is

A. valid.
B. voidable.
C. illegal.
D. void.

124. When subdividers develop subdivisions, they place certain restrictions on each of the lots. Of these, experience has shown which of the following is least likely to be enforced:

A. Minimum size for each lot.
B. Minimum limits on the amount of dollars allowed for improvements on each lot.
C. Minimum limits on the square footage of each home.
D. Limitations on the number of stories or total height of structures.

125. In a timeshare seminar that was advertised to 10,000 people, the timeshare people did not reveal the minimum attendance required for the prize giveaways. Is this a violation of the Real Estate Law?

A. No, the real estate law does not regulate advertising for timeshares.
B. Yes, anyone giving away prizes must disclose in advance the minimum attendance required for the giveaways.
C. No, the law specifically allows the seller of the timeshare to surprise the consumer by requiring attendance at a presentation.
D. Yes, unless the prize is in excess of $10,000.

126. A house sells for $150,000. The buyer assumed an existing loan against the property for $130,000. The documentary transfer tax for this county is $.55 per $500 of consideration. The transfer tax is

A. $11.00.
B. $22.00.
C. $33.00.
D. $44.00.

127. A deposit receipt does not contain the clause that states that in case of buyer default, the broker is entitled to part of the buyer's forfeited deposit. If the buyer defaults, according to this contract the broker is entitled to

A. half the normal commission.
B. no commission.
C. half of the forfeited deposit.
D. his full commission.

128. Under the "Bulk Sales Law," who would assume liability for stock-in-trade if no notice were given?

A. Seller
B. Buyer
C. Broker and creditors
D. Creditors

129. After six lots have been sold in a subdivision, the Real Estate Commissioner was informed of misrepresentation in the sales program. The Commissioner could halt the sale of more lots by

A. voiding the public report.
B. attaching the unsold lots.
C. issuing a Desist and Refrain order.
D. filing an accusation in court.

130. Accrued Depreciation is most nearly

A. a sinking fund.
B. the total depreciation of an improvement to date.
C. the amount of depreciation that takes place in one year.
D. the amount of depreciation that the owner estimates will take place within 10 years.

131. A home was listed for sale for $235,000. The broker was instructed by the owner to accept a deposit on the purchase price of "no less than $1000" and drew up an offer on a standard deposit receipt form. The broker could only get the buyer to submit a $500 deposit. Should the contract later be defaulted by an act of the buyer, the broker would be entitled to

A. 6% of the listing price.
B. up to one-half of the forfeited deposit.
C. one-half of the normal commission.
D. nothing.

132. In a tight money market, under which type of financing would the buyer be most likely required to pay the most loan points?

A. Cal-Vet
B. VA
C. FHA
D. Conventional

133. Baker sold 640 acres of land to Garcia by agreement and deed that provided, "Seller retains rights to all minerals and materials of the earth under this land." Shortly thereafter, while Garcia was preparing his land for cultivation, Baker appeared with oil drilling equipment. Garcia refused to allow him on the land. Baker sued Garcia. Based on the foregoing information, the judge's decision should be

A. Baker has the right to enter on Garcia's land to drill for oil.
B. Baker has no right of entry on Garcia's land.
C. Baker may drill below Garcia's land but must do so from outside its boundaries.
D. Baker may enter Garcia's land only below 500 feet under the surface.

134. If the city acquires land for public streets by dedication, the grantor may seek to have the land returned to him if

A. he simply retakes it; it would be adverse possession.
B. the conveyed easement has been abandoned by the city.
C. the city failed to pay "just compensation."
D. the city fails to maintain the streets.

135. Mr. Parker is holding $300 in an impound account on a Trust Deed on which he has been receiving payments from Mr. Carroll. Which of the following is true concerning the impound account?

A. He may draw interest on the account if placed in a savings and loan association.
B. It should always have a constant balance equal to one year's taxes and insurance.
C. It cannot exceed by more than 5% the amount needed for one year's taxes and insurance.
D. It benefits the trustor and the beneficiary.

136. A real estate broker negotiated a five-year Second Trust Deed loan for $21,000 and charged a $1,500 commission. The maximum commission he could charge legally is

A. $550.
B. $325.
C. $1,650.
D. Any amount agreed upon.

137. Demand is one of the four elements of value. In order for demand to be effective, it must be implemented by the

A. highest and best use.
B. location.
C. purchasing power.
D. amenities.

138. Broker Green obtained a listing from Ms. Brown to sell her home. Ms. Brown told Green the sewers were in and connected and signed a listing to that effect. Green was of the opinion that there were no sewers installed in that street, so he checked with the city and found he was correct. Green showed the house to Jones, who did not ask about sewers, and Green made the sale without any comment. Later, Jones found that the sewers were not in. Which of the following is true?

A. Green had a right to rely on the listing, even though he knew it to be incorrect.
B. Green had a duty to tell Jones, even though Jones did not ask.
C. Jones was to blame because he could have checked with the city—"Caveat Emptor."
D. There is no provision in the law to cover the situation.

139. The interest held by the sublessor when real property is subleased is called a/an

A. assignment.
B. sandwich lease.
C. freehold lease.
D. double lease.

140. Under Federal Income Tax law, the taxpayer could adjust *(increase)* the cost basis on his personal residence for

A. premiums on insurance.
B. cost of a new patio.
C. interest on loans.
D. depreciation.

141. What is the length of the escrow period if there is no provision in the escrow instructions?

A. 60 days
B. 30 days
C. A reasonable time
D. As long as the parties desire

142. Which of the following is a requirement in order for a deed to be valid and convey title?

A. An acknowledgement
B. Execution on a day of the week other than Sunday
C. A property description
D. Use of the phrase "to have and to hold"

143. Which of the following is true with respect to an Impound Account?

A. The lender holding the account pays the same interest rate on the funds as that paid by a savings and loan on savings accounts.
B. It benefits both the trustor and the beneficiary.
C. The maximum amount cannot exceed 5% of the annual disbursements.
D. It is required on all home loans.

144. The head of a family has homesteaded a residence. The market value is $400,000. The balance due on the first trust deed is $335,000. A creditor has petitioned for an execution on the property to satisfy a $2,000 judgment. The creditor

A. cannot obtain redress because the property is a residence.
B. cannot obtain redress because there is insufficient equity to satisfy the judgment.
C. can force a sale of the property because the owner has an equity of $65,000.
D. can force a sale because the market value is greater than the $75,000 exemption.

145. A subdivider purchases 20 acres of land and erects a number of tract homes. She does not hold a real estate license but, to keep things in the family, she wants to pay her son direct for selling the houses. Which of the following statements is true?

A. The son could sell homes in the mother's subdivision and collect a direct commission if he has a salesman's license.
B. The son could sell homes in the mother's subdivision if he has a Real Estate Broker's license.
C. The son needs no real estate license since this is his mother's subdivision.
D. The son must hold a Real Property Securities license.

146. Your neighbor has just built a wall that encroaches a foot onto your property. How long do you have to take action?

A. One year
B. Two years
C. Three years
D. Four years

147. Which of the following could NOT be described as functional obsolescence?

A. Improvements that have lost their usefulness.
B. The proximity of obnoxious nuisances.
C. No air conditioning in a commercial building in a warm climate.
D. Outmoded or outlandish design.

148. The net effect of a tight money policy implemented by the Federal Reserve Board would be the increasing of

A. new home sales.
B. use of new first mortgages in real estate financing.
C. use of junior loans in real estate financing.
D. supply of money available for real estate financing.

149. Which of the following statements is true about listings?

A. A net listing is illegal in California.
B. An exclusive listing may be for a period of 30 days.
C. An exclusive listing may be for a period of 24 hours.
D. Both B and C are correct.

150. A township is

A. 8 square miles.
B. 36 sections.
C. Larger than a range.
D. 1 square mile.

151. When owners of real property hold title as Tenants in Common

A. The one who lives the longest always winds up as the sole owner.
B. The individual owners give up their right to will their interest in the property.
C. Each of the co-owners' interest may be conveyed separately.
D. All co-owners must own an equal interest in the property.

152. Who pays the points on a Cal-Vet loan?

A. Buyer
B. Seller
C. State of California
D. No one

153. A real estate broker advertises that he will give a television valued at $500 to any buyer who purchases a property listed for sale with his office. This type of advertisement is considered to be

A. legal only if the gift value is $100 or less.
B. legal if the seller is mailed a copy of the advertisement.
C. legal if proper disclosure is made to all interested parties.
D. illegal even if full disclosure is made to all interested parties.

154. A Mechanic's Lien differs from a Judgment in which respect?

A. A Judgment is not valid unless recorded.
B. A Mechanic's Lien is a statutory lien based upon a constitutional provision.
C. A Mechanic's Lien becomes unenforceable after a lapse of time.
D. Anyone having an interest in the property has the right, anytime after the claim is due and before the right of redemption has expired, to discharge a Mechanic's Lien by satisfying the claim.

155. When an Abstract of Judgment is recorded it becomes a/an

A. specific lien against the property involved.
B. easement on the property involved.
C. general lien on all non-exempt real property in the county where recorded.
D. attachment lien on the property involved.

156. For property tax assessment purposes, the county assessor would consider a new well and pump installed on a parcel of land to be

A. part of the land.
B. personal property.
C. additions.
D. improvements.

157. Townships running north and south of a baseline are called

A. ranges.
B. rows.
C. tiers.
D. layers.

158. The secondary mortgage market relates to

A. federal policing of the savings and loan associations.
B. junior liens.
C. participation in real estate financing by out-of-state lenders.
D. transfers of mortgages between lenders or investors.

159. Your land is taken for a freeway. This is done under laws

A. concerning police power of the state.
B. relating to eminent domain.
C. of dedication.
D. concerning easements.

160. An individual who holds a leasehold estate has a

A. fee simple estate.
B. remainder.
C. reversion.
D. chattel real.

161. Life insurance companies not willing to deal directly with mortgagors/trustors usually pay a loan preparation and servicing fee, and make real estate mortgage loans to purchasers indirectly through

A. savings and loan associations.
B. FHA or VA.
C. mortgage companies.
D. all of the above.

162. Provisions of the State Housing Act are enforced by

A. the Real Estate Commissioner.
B. California Department of Fair Housing and Employment.
C. FHA and VA.
D. HUD.

163. Easements are terminated by all of the following, except

A. prescription by the owner of the servient tenement.
B. merger of the dominant and servient tenement.
C. revocation by the owner of the servient tenement.
D. release by the owner of the dominant tenement.

164. A lease is to a lessee as a/an

A. assumption agreement is to an affiant.
B. trust deed is to a trustee.
C. agreement of sale is to an equitable owner.
D. fee simple estate is to an executor.

165. An attachment lien placed on real property can be released by all of the following EXCEPT

A. court order.
B. death of the defendant.
C. written release by the plaintiff.
D. satisfaction of judgment provided it is in favor of the plaintiff.

166. If a real estate broker as an agent does not follow the lawful instructions of his principal he

A. is liable to his principal for damages.
B. is subject to a fine or imprisonment.
C. could lose his license in a court of competent jurisdiction.
D. any of the above.

167. The following statement is FALSE in reference to alcoholic beverage licenses

A. an alien can hold an on-sale general license.
B. an alien can hold an off-sale general license.
C. licenses may not be pledged as security for a loan.
D. wholesalers can also hold a retailer's on-sale license.

168. A subdivider must satisfy the requirements of the Department of Real Estate if the property offered for sale in California is located

A. outside of California.
B. within the city and county identified in a recorded map.
C. within California.
D. in any of the above.

169. Julie enters into a contract with Alan under duress and is in fear for her safety if she does not sign. The contract is

A. valid.
B. void.
C. voidable.
D. unenforceable.

170. The legal meaning of the word waiver as it is applied to real estate transactions most nearly means

A. estoppel.
B. the justifiable reliance by one party upon the intentional act or omission of another.
C. a unilateral act and its legal consequences.
D. detrimental reliance.

171. Mrs. Gross "homesteaded" her family's dwelling. No prior "homestead" had been recorded by either spouse. The property had a first trust deed with a balance of $300,000 and was worth $360,000. A general creditor later obtained a judgment for $2,000. The judgment was

A. collectible because the wife was not the "head of family" and therefore could not record a valid homestead.
B. collectible the because wife's homestead gave only $10,000 exemption from execution and the judgment lien would be paid out of the balance of the equity.
C. not collectible since the wife's homestead was valid and the homestead exemption left no equity upon which to levy.
D. not collectible since a general creditor's judgment is always inferior to a homestead exemption.

172. Prescription is

A. equitable title.
B. legal title.
C. a grant.
D. the right to use another person's land.

173. If the owner of real property carries proper fire insurance coverage, that insurance policy will protect the owner in the event of loss. In such a case, the insured

A. might gain, but definitely will not lose money.
B. should neither gain nor lose.
C might lose, but certainly will not gain.
D. none of the above.

174. Smith purchased an older apartment house as her first real estate investment. This property had several owners and they all claimed depreciation deductions on their federal income tax returns because of the subject property. When Smith files her return, she can depreciate the property

A. based on the purchase price of the land and improvements.
B. Without regard to the total depreciation deducted in the past.
C. if she makes allowance for the depreciation taken by prior owners.
D. provided she uses the same economic life as the first owner of the property.

175. A definition of value to an appraiser is

A. the ability of one commodity to command other commodities in exchange.
B. the present worth of future benefits arising out of ownership of a property.
C. a relationship between desirous persons and things desired.
D. any of the above.

176. Of the following, which would be the least likely place to acquire a loan on a single-family residence?

A Bank
B Savings and loan
C. Insurance company
D. Mortgage company

177. Regarding Mortgage Insurance Premiums, they benefit the

A. lender in case of default of the borrower.
B. lender in case of death of the borrower.
C. borrower in case of death.
D. lender against delinquency in payments.

178. Under the Law of Agency, a fiduciary relationship is created between the broker and the seller upon execution of the listing agreement. As far as the broker's responsibility to third parties, the broker

A. must be fair and honest.
B. has no obligation.
C. need only disclose material facts when asked about them.
D. should disclose the lowest price the seller is willing to accept.

179. Which of the following can the Federal Reserve Board do if they feel that there is an inflationary trend developing in the United States?

A Increase the discount rate
B. Enter into the government bond market in a selling capacity
C. Adjust the amount of reserves required for its member banks
D. All of the above.

180. The Statute of Frauds does not apply to

A. a listing contract to sell real property.
B. a general partnership formed to invest in real property.
C. a commission agreement concerning the sale of real property.
D. real property leased for a period of two years.

181. When real property is held by husband and wife as community property, an agreement to sell that property that has been signed by only one spouse would be considered to be

A. illegal.
B. unenforceable.
C. binding.
D. a violation of the Statute of Frauds.

182. Effective Gross Income is the

A. spendable income after taxes.
B. gross income minus allowable expenses and payments of principal and interest.
C. gross income minus an allowance for vacancies.
D. gross income minus allowable expenses and depreciation.

183. In the case of a sale, which of the following would be exempt from the "Discrimination and Unlawful Acts" chapter in the Health and Safety Code?

A. Owner occupied residence financed by the VA.
B. Four-plex financed by FHA.
C. Owner occupied single residence unencumbered.
D. None of the above.

184. When commercial real estate is purchased today, the minimum period of time over which the owner can depreciate the improvements is

A. 15 years.
B. 27 1/2 years.
C. 39 years.
D. 42 years.

185. Equity in real property is the

A. cash flow value.
B. total of all mortgage payments made to date.
C. difference between mortgage indebtedness and market value.
D. appraised value.

186. A real estate broker advertises that he will give a microwave oven valued at $500 to anyone who purchases a property listed with his office. This type of advertisement is

A. legal only if the gift is valued at $100 or less.
B. legal if the seller is sent a copy of the advertisement.
C. legal if proper disclosures are made to all parties of interest.
D. illegal regardless if all disclosures are made.

187. When rent is computed on the gross sales of a business occupying real property, the lease is correctly termed a

A. net lease.
B. gross lease.
C. voidable lease.
D. percentage lease.

188. The real estate commissioner would prohibit which of the following mortgage broker advertisements?

A. We loan up to 75% of verified market value.
B. We loan upon verification of equity.
C. Call 1-800-For-A-Loan.
D. First trust deeds available - 10% APR.

189. A lender plans to make a construction loan for the construction of 10 homes in a new subdivision. He wants to make certain that his loan has the first priority of any liens. He would LEAST likely

A. make a personal inspection of the land.
B. post and record a notice of non-responsibility.
C. require an ALTA policy.
D. require a copy of the Commissioner's final public report.

190. In valuing a single-family home, the appraiser discovered an assessment lien for $4,000 for sewer and street improvement bonds. The appraiser located several recent sales of similar residences for $600,000 each, none of which had the assessment lien. The indicated value of the subject property would be

A. $596,000.
B. $600,000.
C. $604,000.
D. none of the above.

191. If a real estate licensee was trying to persuade people to list or to sell their property by telling them that members of another ethnic group were moving into their neighborhood, and it would be to their advantage to list or to sell, it would be an example of all of the following, EXCEPT

A. blockbusting.
B. panic selling.
C. illegal conduct.
D. legitimate conduct.

192. The replacement cost approach is easier to apply to a new building due to

A. building code changes.
B. historic costs being hard to obtain.
C. land valuation problems.
D. depreciation estimates.

193. Which of the following is not "real property"?

A. Airspace above property
B. Fences
C. Trees
D. Trust deed

194. A will, which is entirely written, dated, and signed in the testator's own handwriting, is a

A. witnessed will.
B. holographic will.
C. nuncupative will.
D. probate will.

195. The term "Et Ux" refers to

A. "And others."
B. "In the will."
C. "And wife."
D. None of the above.

196. Single-family home values are least protected in neighborhoods where there is a/an

A. similarity of income of the owners.
B. predominance of residents belonging to the same ethnic or religious group affiliation.

C. minimum of change to existing restrictions as a result of legal restrictions.
D. increasing mixture of average-quality homes with high-quality homes.

197. An investment that was purchased as a hedge against inflation would best be exemplified by which of the following?

A. An investment that will have the characteristics of an annuity.
B. An income-producing investment that will maintain its value.
C. A risk-free investment.
D. An investment that will afford a high degree of liquidity.

198. An Abstract of Title is most similar to a

A. Chain of Title.
B. Title Search.
C. Preliminary Title Report.
D. Standard policy of Title Insurance.

199. A partnership may take title to real property in

A. the name of the partnership.
B. the individual names of one or more partners.
C. the name of a third party as trustee for the partnership.
D. any of the above ways.

200. All of the following items are usually prorated at the close of escrow, except

A. homeowner's insurance.
B. property taxes and assessments.
C. delinquent interest on unsecured loans.
D. interest and impounds.

201. A Subdivision Public Report is good

A. for one year.
B. until a material change should take place.
C. until the final public report is issued.
D. Any of the above.

202. Which of the following is a legal contract that gives the holder rights to enjoyment and use of another's property short of an estate?

A. A life estate
B. An easement
C. A less than freehold estate
D. An estate for years

203. A corporation built a large tract of homes in a new subdivision and hired a handy man to take care of any maintenance or repairs that might arise. He was given additional compensation for showing the homes on weekends to prospective buyers. Under these circumstances:

A. The corporation was within its rights and there is no violation of the Real Estate Law.
B. The maintenance man could be fined for showing the homes without a real estate license.
C. The handy man does not need a real estate license because he is an employee of a corporate owner.
D. All corporation employees and officers selling the property must be licensed.

204. Who signs a "Deed of Reconveyance"?

A. Trustor
B. Trustee

C. Beneficiary
D. Grantor

205. The zoning symbol for multiple family dwellings is

A. C-4.
B. R-3.
C. R-1-40.
D. M-1.

206. An Abstract of Judgment for money awarded by a court becomes which of the following, when duly recorded in the county where the property of the judgment debtor is located?

A. An involuntary lien
B. A voluntary lien
C. An equitable lien
D. An attached lien

207. A survey that refers to fractional sections, townships and ranges is a legal description by

A. metes and bounds.
B. recorded map.
C. U.S. Government Survey.
D. none of the above.

208. Irons, a 15-year-old emancipated minor, entered into a listing contract with a broker to sell property that he owned. When the broker finds a buyer, and both parties have signed a purchase contract, the broker should obtain proof of the emancipation to satisfy the demands of the

A. escrow holder.
B. title company.
C. buyer.
D. buyer's broker.

209. Which would all be specific liens?

A. Judgment lien, federal estate tax lien, corporation franchise tax lien.
B. Federal income tax lien attachment, surety bail bond lien.
C. Vendor's lien, lien for a decedent's debts, vendee's lien.
D. Mechanic's lien, property tax lien, mortgages and attachments.

210. Which of the following represents a gross misrepresentation by an agent?

A. The representation is an obvious falsehood.
B. The representation is made with the knowledge of a falsehood.
C. The representation caused the aggrieved party to enter into the contract.
D. All of the above.

211. In a business opportunity transaction, the document that is used in the same manner as a deed in a real estate transaction is the

A. financing Statement.
B. bill of Sale.
C. trust Deed.
D. chattel Mortgage.

212. A real estate broker could make any of the following statements about land contracts and be correct, EXCEPT

A. conveyance of title is not required within one year.
B. title must be passed at the time a deed is delivered.
C. the contract signatures must be acknowledged by the buyer and the seller.
D. the contract must include a statement prohibiting recording.

213. All of the following statements are correct concerning the transfer of title to personal property, EXCEPT

A. title to personal property can be transferred by the delivery of possession.
B. the condition of the title to personal property can usually be determined by a study of public records with about the same accuracy as title to real property.
C. personal property is usually considered to be situated in the domicile of the owner regardless of where the property actually is, and is covered by the law that covers the owner's domicile.
D. a written instrument can be used along with the transfer of personal property, but in many cases, such an instrument is not necessary to the validity of the transfer.

214. A broker may not lawfully collect a commission from both buyer and seller without

A. an exclusive listing signed by both parties.
B. notifying both after sale is made.
C. making a sales agreement.
D. the knowledge and consent of both parties prior to the sale.

215. The liquidity of a business refers to the ratio between

A. fixed assets and fixed liabilities.
B. current assets and current liabilities.
C. total capital and total liabilities.
D. net income and gross income.

216. Which of the following lenders is the newest source of funds for real estate financing?

A. Pension funds
B. Commercial banks
C. Savings and loan associations
D. Insurance companies

217. Which of the following would NOT be considered a prime tenant in a shopping center?

A. A chain five-and-dime store
B. A specialty shop
C. A grocery store
D. A department store

218. A person unable to take an oath would take or do which of the following?

A. A confirmation
B. An affirmation
C. An affidavit
D. A notarization

219. Three parties owned equal interests in a large parcel of potentially agricultural land as tenants-in-common. One of the co-owners decided to lease the entire parcel to a third party for agricultural purposes without the consent of the other co-tenants. Under these circumstances, if the two parties entered into the contract, the lease would be

A. valid and binding on the three co-tenants.
B. invalid, as land owned by multiple owners cannot be leased.
C. valid, provided it did not exceed the legal limit of 51 years.
D. invalid, as one co-tenant cannot obligate the other co-tenants for a lease of the whole property without their consent.

220. Which of the following has the least influence on the lending policies of financial institutions that make real estate mortgage loans?

A. Borrower's current income.
B. Present and potential value of the property.
C. Borrower's need for financial assistance.
D. Relative attractiveness of other investments.

221. Which of the following would not be considered essential to making an appraisal of an old family residence?

A. Physical condition of the building
B. Suitability of the residence to the site
C. Original cost of the residence
D. Purpose of the appraisal

222. Under the mortgage loan broker law, the maximum commission that may be charged for negotiating a second or other junior trust deed or mortgage of $4,500 to run for a period of 2 1/2 years is

A. 5%
B. 10%
C. 15%
D. None of the above.

223. There are three approaches to the valuation of real property and if possible all three should be used in arriving at a final estimate of value. Depending on the type of property being appraised, however, one approach will have more weight and should afford authority. The comparison approach is given greater weight in the appraisal of

A. apartment property.
B. service property.
C. single-family dwellings.
D. industrial property.

224. A real estate broker agreed to accept the commission in the form of acres of land that had been appraised by two independent appraisers at $200 per acre. After the close of escrow, the real estate broker was contacted by a potential buyer, with whom the broker had never had any previous contact, who was interested in purchasing the land for $500 per acre. Should the sale be consummated by this buyer? This action would

A. indicate no legal or ethical violation.
B. not be considered illegal, but would be unethical.
C. be illegal and unethical.
D. constitute a violation of the California Real Estate Commissioner's Regulations.

225. During a period of time in which unemployment is declining and the gross national product is increasing:

A. The value of single family residences would tend to increase in value.
B. New home sales would tend to increase.
C. Demand for existing housing would increase.
D. All of the above would be true.

226. The term "megalopolis" best describes which of the following?

A. A giant utility company.
B. A major subdivision.
C. A group of cities.
D. The sum total of all suburbs surrounding the major city.

227. Townsend purchased a property at 20% less than the listed price and later sold it for the original listed price. Townsend's percentage of profit was

A. 10%.
B. 20%.
C. 25%.
D. 40%.

228. In order to bring court action to collect a commission earned for negotiating a month-to-month rental, the broker

A. must have a written listing signed by the owner of the property.
B. could not have charged more than 25% of the first month's rent for his services.
C. must have been registered with the Department of Real Estate as a rental broker.
D. need prove only an oral agreement to pay a commission.

229. A brother and sister purchased property as joint tenants. Later, the sister married, and deeded her interest to herself and her husband. Which of the following statements is correct?

A. The joint tenancy continues to exist in all three persons.
B. The brother remains as a joint tenant.
C. The joint tenancy is terminated.
D. The sister's deed to her husband is voidable by the brother.

230. Which of the following methods would be least effective in appraising a lot on which the buyer wants to build a house?

A. Cost
B. Comparison
C. Income
D. Market value

231. Usually, an escrow officer is authorized to

A. determine which financing is best for the buyer.
B. change the escrow instructions when asked to by the selling agent.
C. call for the funding of the buyer's loan.
D. choose the pest control company.

232. A form that is usually prepared to allow a real estate licensee to act as an agent for all principal parties to the transaction involved is a/an

A. agreement of sale.
B. exchange agreement.
C. loan broker's statement.
D. real property securities statement.

233. A subdivider and developer purchased considerable acreage and now plan to construct a tract of 40 homes. In arranging the financing for the new construction, the lender has agreed to advance part of the funds immediately, and will release a set amount of additional money as each home is completed. The funds that will be forthcoming as construction progresses are known as

A. obligatory advances.
B. reconveyance funds.
C. release monies.
D. open end mortgage payments.

234. A person who acquires real property through intestate succession does so as a result of

A. a formal or witnessed will.
B. a holographic will.
C. a nuncupative will.
D. direction by a probate court.

235. You sell a note with a face value of $12,000 for $10,000. You are

A. discounting the note.
B. amortizing the note.
C. committing an act requiring a real estate license.
D. committing fraud.

236. In appraisal practice, all of the following are accepted methods of computing the estimate of a building cost, EXCEPT the

A. development method
B. quantity survey method
C. unit-in-place cost method
D. cubic foot method

237. An owner of a five-unit apartment building that is located within the city limits intends to convert the building into five condominium units and offer them for sale to the public. Under these circumstances, the developer

A. must obtain a public report from the Real Estate Commissioner under the Subdivided Lands Act.
B. must file a map with the city under the provisions of the Subdivided Map Act.
C. is exempt from the Subdivided Lands Act and the Subdivision Map Act.
D. must comply with the Subdivided Lands Act and the Subdivision Map Act.

238. Which of the following is a legal term used to describe the entire parcel of real property and all structures on such property?

A. Condominium
B. Condominium unit
C. Condominium project
D. All of the above.

239. A lender of money on real property should be relatively certain that her mortgage is an enforceable lien. She can best accomplish this by

A. recordation.
B. a title insurance policy.
C. providing for an acceleration clause.
D. a physical inspection of the property.

240. Of the following factors, which would not contribute to obsolescence?

A. Wear and tear from use
B. Out-of-date equipment
C. Change of locational demand
D. Misplacement of improvement

241. Compared to the return from investments from other areas, the return from real property should be

A. equal to the return from first trust deeds.
B. equal to the return from bonds.
C. higher than the return from bonds and first trust deeds.
D. higher than the return from bonds but less than the return from first trust deeds.

242. Mutual mortgage insurance would be included in the issuance of a/an

A. conventional loan.
B. Cal-Vet loan.
C. FHA loan assumption.
D. VA backed loan.

243. Which of the following best describes a "complete" escrow?

A It is considered a perfect escrow.
B. The escrow holder has ceased being an agent for both parties.
C. All papers are properly drawn up and ready for final steps to be taken to close the escrow.

D. All services of the escrow holder are involved.

244. "Tax shelter" as referred to by a real estate broker is

A. an installment sale of property.
B. a tax deferred exchange.
C. depreciation.
D. any of the above.

245. In reference to the California Land Title Association Policy of title insurance: the advantage of having an extended coverage as opposed to standard coverage is

A. physical aspects.
B. government regulations.
C. forgery.
D. lack of capacity.

246. Which of the following ways of compensating real property managers is not proper business practice?

A. Commission on new leases
B. Receipt of discounts on purchases or supplies
C. Percentage of gross receipts
D. Commission on major repairs or alterations

247. From a lender's point of view, the most significant feature of a purchase-money mortgage is that it takes priority over

A. any seller's liens.
B. tax liens.
C. any liens against the purchaser that exist at time of purchase.
D. all liens existing at the time of sale.

248. Mary Johnson looks at a property while her husband is out of town on a business trip. Mary feels this is the perfect property, and is afraid someone else will buy the property before her husband returns. She puts a deposit down on the home and signs the deposit receipt. How should the contract be signed?

A. John Johnson and Mary Johnson, by Mary Johnson.
B. John Johnson and Mary Johnson, Husband and Wife.
C. The Johnsons by Mary Johnson.
D. Mary Johnson.

249. An undivided interest with the right of survivorship is called

A. tenancy in severalty.
B. tenancy in common.
C. joint tenancy.
D. none of the above.

250. Which of the following is NOT essential to a valid deed?

A. Acknowledgment of the grantor's signature
B. In writing
C. Signed by the grantor
D. Competent grantor

251. A property owner seeking protection against mechanics liens would file a notice

A. of summation.
B. of nonresponsibility.
C. to quit.
D. to cease and desist.

252. A deed that is not dated or recorded is

A. invalid.
B. unenforceable.
C. valid.
D. A and B are correct.

253. An easement on real property can be terminated by

A. a conveyance of the servient tenement to a third party.
B. being revoked by the party granting the easement.
C. an express release from the servient tenement holder.
D. a release signed by the holder of the dominant tenement.

254. The legitimacy of zoning laws rests upon the

A. fact that planning boards are local, and thus close to the people they regulate.
B. established right of police power of government.
C. ease of enforcing them.
D. fact that their enforcement does not interfere with interstate commerce.

255. In connection with FHA insured loans, lenders charge points in order to

A. obtain the market yield.
B. close the gap between the market rate and fixed rates.
C. increase the effective yield.
D. all of the above.

256. The following would be an estate in real property

A. an easement
B. privilege to use another's property
C. a lease
D. all of the above.

257. Which of the following is represented by the symbol of an equal sign (=) inside a house?

A. Equal Housing Opportunity
B. Society of Residential Appraisers
C. Home Builders Institute
D. Build America Better

258. A real estate broker has a valid listing on a property. He places a classified advertisement containing only the following information - "4 bedroom, 2 bathroom home with swimming pool. Asking price $270,000. Telephone 555-2466." This kind of advertisement is an example of a

A. blind ad.
B. display ad.
C. qualified ad.
D. quiet ad.

259. A real estate broker generally acts

A. in a dual agency.
B. as a fiduciary.
C. by ratification.
D. as an ostensible agent.

260. Of the following agreements select the one that is NOT required to be in writing under the provisions of the Statute of Frauds?

A. An agreement authorizing an agent to purchase or sell real estate for compensation.
B. An agreement that by its terms is not to be performed within a year of the making thereof.
C. A general partnership agreement to deal in real property.

D. An agreement for the leasing for a period of time longer than one year, or for the sale of real property or of an interest therein.

261. In working with subdivided property for which the Commissioner's Preliminary Public Report has been issued, a licensee may

A. accept an offer to purchase and take a deposit awaiting approval of Commissioner's final report.
B. take a listing on the property.
C. take an exclusive listing without a termination date since it is uncertain how long it will take to sell all of the lots.
D. lease the property, but not sell it.

262. When subdividers develop subdivisions, they place certain restrictions on each of the lots. Of these, experience has shown one of the following is least likely to be enforced:

A. Minimum size for each lot
B. Minimum limits on the amount of dollars allowed for improvements on each lot
C. Minimum limits on the square footage of each home
D. Limitations on the number of stories or total height of structures

263. In arriving at an estimate of value, an appraiser would be most interested in which date?

A. The date that the purchase contract was signed.
B. The date that the deed was recorded.
C. The date that the sale went into escrow.
D. The date that the escrow was closed.

264. Which of the following would be the best and most complete definition of the term "encumbrance"?

A. An interest possessed by a stranger to the title that affects the estate but does not affect the owners from enjoying and transferring the fee.
B. That which is attached to the land.
C. A legalized lien.
D. The ability of any stranger to walk across your property even if you did not want him to.

265. A licensed real estate broker who owned a large real estate firm operating under the name of ABC Realty Company listed a property for a total price of $450,000. The broker and many of his salespersons were all principals in an investment company operating under the name of Realty Income Investment Company. The investment company decided to purchase the property so the broker presented all cash offers to the owner for the full price but did not disclose to the seller who the purchasers were. The seller accepted the offer and opened escrow. Under these circumstances the

A. broker's actions were perfectly legal since he offered the full cash price.
B. broker's offer would be legal provided he added to the escrow instructions the fact that the purchasing firm was composed of brokers and salespersons.
C. broker acted properly provided he had agreed to waive any commission.
D. broker's action was improper because he did not reveal the true identity of the purchaser.

266. Assume that after an offer to purchase has been accepted by a seller and it later develops that the first trust deed that the buyer is taking over is for only $120,000 instead of $140,000, as indicated in the listing contract. In this case

A. the buyer must go through with the transaction or lose his deposit money and be subject to suit for specific performance.
B. this situation is to the buyer's advantage as it automatically reduces the price of the property by $20,000.
C. the seller can force the buyer to increase the amount of the second trust deed to take care of the discrepancy.
D. the buyer can rescind the contract and recover his deposit.

267. A Lis Pendens action is effective

A. until the judgment rendered has become final.
B. only until commencement of court proceedings.
C. through the period of court proceedings and rendering of judgment only.
D. five years from date of filing action.

268. Property is

A. personal if not real.
B. real if a fixture.
C. personal if a lease agreement.
D. all of the above.

269. Which of these is not considered an estate in real property?

A. Leasehold
B. Remainder
C. Trust deed
D. Estoppel

270. Which of the following court cases ruled upon in the United States Supreme Court in 1968 has had far-reaching effects upon recent legislative acts and court rulings throughout the country, prohibiting "racial" discrimination in the sale and rental of housing?

A. Lawrence vs. Pann
B. Jones vs. Mayer
C. Bidwell vs. Smith
D. Smith vs. Kramer

271. When considering interior decoration, which of the following statements would be incorrect?

A. Dark colors make a room look larger.
B. Beige, white and cream are cool colors.
C. Walls and woodwork painted the same color make the rooms seem larger.
D. Natural wood doors are more luxurious than painted doors.

272. When examining a properly prepared closing statement, the broker would discover that a mortgage assumed by the buyer would appear as

A. a debit to the buyer.
B. a debit to the seller.
C. a credit to the seller.
D. none of the above.

273. RESPA (the Real Estate Settlement Procedures Act) regulates lenders to which of the following?

A. One-to-four family residential dwellings
B. Common interest subdivisions
C. Commercial property
D. Industrial real estate only

274. Which of the following would be classified as "boot" in a tax-free exchange?

A. Another property that is unlike
B. Mortgage relief
C. Cash
D. All of the above.

275. The maximum commission that can be charged by a licensee for negotiating a Second Trust Deed of $7,000 for a five-year term is

A. 5%.
B. 10%.
C. 15%.
D. unlimited.

276. Broker Johnson sold property to a principal who was under 18 years of age and a minor. The broker did not know this until the property went to escrow. The contract is

A. illegal.
B. valid.
C. void.
D. voidable.

277. The minimum time that must run after publication of a notice to creditors, under the provisions of the Uniform Commercial Code pertaining to bulk sales, before consummation of the sale is _____ days.

A. 5
B. 10
C. 12
D. 15

278. Private restrictions on land can be created by

A. deed.
B. written agreement.
C. general plan restrictions in subdivisions.
D. all of the above.

279. A judgment that has been recorded would be a/an

A. involuntary lien.
B. superior lien.
C. equitable lien.
D. inferior lien.

280. The California Fair Housing Act is also known as

A. Rumford Act.
B. Unruh Act.
C. Title VIII.
D. F.E.P.C.

281. Most of the junior loans that are secured by real property are secured through

A. private investors.
B. savings and loan associations.
C. commercial banks.
D. credit unions.

282. Which of the following forms of ownership always consists of an undivided interest with the rights of survivorship?

A. Joint tenancy
B. Community property
C. Severalty
D. Tenancy in common

283. The value of a property purchased for investment purposes is usually

A. based on the capitalization of future net income.
B. inversely proportional to the remaining economic life of the building.
C. determined by a gross multiplier factor.
D. proportional to the structural soundness of the building.

284. The five requisites for a land contract are

A. mutuality, consideration, offer/acceptance, legality, legal object.
B. legality, capacity of the parties, offer/acceptance, writing, mutuality.
C. mutuality, capacity of the parties, writing, offer/acceptance, consideration.
D. consideration, legality, offer/acceptance, capacity of the parties, writing.

285. Growing crops would be placed as security for a loan using which one of the following documents?

A. A trust deed
B. A security agreement
C. A bill of sale
D. A notice of sale

286. An easement differs from a license in that a license

A. must be created by written instrument.
B. is of indefinite duration.
C. may be assigned.
D. may be revoked.

287. An attorney-in-fact with general powers can do all of the following except

A. sign the name of his principal.
B. perform certain acts under a general power of attorney.
C. deal in real estate without recording his power of attorney.
D. encumber his principal's property with a trust deed wherein some other person is the beneficiary.

288. Regarding parks, playgrounds, and public buildings owned by the city, title is held

A. as community property.
B. as a tenant in common.
C. in severalty.
D. in joint tenancy.

289. An owner of commercial property entered into separate open listing contracts with a number of different real estate brokers. Under these circumstances, each broker will:

A. Have an opportunity to earn a full commission if he or she is the procuring cause.
B. Equally share the commission if any one of the brokers sells the property.
C. Earn a full commission if the owner sells the property herself.
D. Have the right to exercise an option to purchase the property at the listed price.

290. If prices rise 20%, what happens to the purchasing power of the dollar?

A. It has gone down 10%.
B. It has gone down 16 2/3%.
C. It has gone down 20%.
D. Nothing, the purchasing power of the dollar is unchanged.

291. The largest area would be

A. 10% of a township.
B. One mile by one mile.
C. Two sections.
D. 5280 feet by 5280 feet.

292. The lending institution that is permitted by law to offer the longest pay-off period on a conventional loan is the

A. mutual savings bank.
B. insurance company.
C. savings and loan association.
D. commercial bank.

293. Which of the following is not real property?

A. Airspace over an airfield.
B. Newly planted ornamental trees.
C. Stock in a real estate corporation.
D. Minerals in the ground.

294. A seller of a home suffered damages due to misrepresentations made by the broker with whom the seller had been dealing. In the lawsuit filed against the broker by the seller, the broker contended that he was not liable since the listing contract had been an oral and not a written agreement as required under the statute of frauds. Under these circumstances the court would likely rule that:

A. Since the contract was not in writing, the statute of frauds would relieve the broker of any liability.
B. The broker would not be liable for any damages if escrow had closed before damages had been established.
C. The broker is liable and the statute of frauds is not the issue.
D. The broker is only liable if the misrepresentations had been given in written form.

295. Mortgages and other lien instruments are considered

A. chattels real.
B. personal property exclusively.
C. to create an estate in real property.
D. to create less-than-freehold estates.

296. If a spouse leases the residence owned by the husband and wife as community property for one year, without the consent of the spouse, the contract is

A. unenforceable.
B. void, since the wife did not sign.
C. valid and enforceable.
D. voidable.

297. Economic life of an improvement depends on

A. owner's repair policy.
B. use of the improvement.
C. condition and age of the improvement.
D. all of the above.

298. The Uniform Commercial Code, Division 6, which pertains to bulk sale transfer of business goods, exists primarily for the protection of

A. buyers.
B. sellers.
C. creditors.
D. silent partners.

299. Most junior loans negotiated are secured from

A. insurance companies.
B. savings and loan associations.
C. private lenders.
D. commercial banks.

300. An example of a device hypothecating real property as security is the:

A. grant deed.
B. promissory note.
C. trust deed.
D. none of these.

301. A prudent investor, to hedge against the erosion of capital caused by inflation, would logically place funds in

A. government bonds.
B. real property.
C. trust deeds and mortgages.
D. saving accounts.

302. Which of the following can be insured by a title insurance company?

A. The validity of an easement
B. Loss due to an undesirable clause in private restrictions
C. The validity of a tenant's lease interest free from liens and encumbrances
D. All of the above.

303. In order to hold real property as tenants in common, individuals must

A. hold undivided interests.
B. hold equal interests.
C. be husband and wife.
D. arrange for possession.

304. A lender referring to a "Seasoned Loan" would be talking about a loan

A. made during a particular season of the year.
B. with a previous pattern of prompt payments.
C. on which a due date has been extended.
D. where additional sums may be advanced at a later date.

305. In which of the following situations would the Attorney General of California become involved?

A. Investigation into fraudulent real estate subdivisions.
B. The legality of licensing procedures.
C. A broker whose license has been suspended brings court action against the Real Estate Commissioner to overturn the decision.
D. All of the above.

306. Katz made full payment on a note secured by a deed of trust on his property, and he demanded that the beneficiary clear the records. The beneficiary must move for a reconveyance

A. within a reasonable time.
B. if the trustee does not do so.
C. immediately.
D. within 30 days.

307. The level of mortgage interest rates is directly affected by all of the following except

A. inflation rate.
B. unemployment rate.
C. supply and demand.
D. demand for funds.

308. An appraiser's first step in estimating value on a piece of vacant land is to assess

A. original cost of land.
B. price the owner now thinks it is worth.
C. highest and best use.
D. prices of vacant comparables.

309. A broker belonged to a real estate syndicate. He had a listing on an apartment house that he felt would be a good investment for his syndicate. He consulted with the syndicate and the members agreed. The syndicate purchased the apartment house, but when the seller found out that the broker was involved in the purchase and hadn't told him about this, the seller refused to go through with the sale. The broker sued the seller for his commission claiming he had found a buyer "ready, willing and able." The courts would probably

A. make the seller sell and pay the broker his full commission.
B. rule in favor of the seller.
C. pay the broker one half of his commission.
D. fine the broker $10,000 and sentence him to five years in a state prison.

310. Interest paid on top of interest is

A. straight interest.
B. compound interest.
C. amortized interest.
D. double interest.

311. The fact that no two parcels of land are exactly alike is one of the basis for courts of law to enforce

A. Lis Pendens.
B. Partition Action.
C. Specific Performance.
D. Quiet Title Action.

312. According to the provisions of both federal and state civil rights legislation, discrimination due to race, color, creed or national origin in housing is

A. unenforceable.
B. unlawful.
C. illegal.
D. all of the above.

313. No subdivision lots in an unincorporated area of a California county can be legally sold or leased prior to

A. furnishing a copy of the Commissioner's Final Public Report to the customer.
B. giving the customer a chance to read it.
C. obtaining the signature of the customer for a copy of the report.
D. all of the above.

314. Liquidation of an obligation on an installment basis means

A. annexation.
B. amortization.
C. acceleration.
D. condemnation.

315. The unit of comparison when using the market data approach of appraisal on a single-family residence is the

A. square foot.
B. cubic foot.
C. capitalization rate.
D. entire property.

316. If a property with a $2,400 gross monthly income sold with an annual gross rent multiplier of 10.72, what is the sales price?

A. $250,000
B. $280,000
C. $295,640
D. $308,736

317. If a broker has a nonexclusive listing and he wants to be legally entitled to a commission, he must be able to prove that

A. he was a duly licensed broker at the time of the transaction.
B. he found a buyer who was ready, willing, and able to buy.
C. he was the procuring cause of the sale.
D. all of the above.

318. The comparison method of appraising would be least reliable

A. in an inactive market.
B. in a neighborhood where the land uses are rapidly changing.
C. when the comparables are in the same price range.
D. when the comparables are located in another neighborhood.

319. In FHA financing as opposed to conventional financing, the lender's main benefit is the

A. mortgage insurance.
B. higher loan to value ration.
C. higher yield.
D. ease of sale in the secondary money market.

320. "A" owns a parcel of real property free and clear of all encumbrances, and has leased one of the apartments therein to "B." Thereafter, "B" sublets the apartment to "C." In view of the above

A. "B" has assigned his entire right, title and interest in and to the leasehold.
B. "B" has transferred his entire leasehold to "C."
C. "C" is now liable to pay the apartment rent to "A."
D. "A" can hold "B" liable for the rent if "C" does not pay.

321. The basis of the market data approach to appraising is found in the principle of

A. change.
B. substitution.
C. conformity.
D. anticipation.

322. Two of the most important things for a borrower to be advised about under the "Truth in Lending" law are:

A. Disclosure and discount rate.
B. Finance charge and annual percentage rate.
C. Carrying charge and advertising.
D. Installment payments and cancellation rights.

323. Which of the following would be an advantage in the ownership of income-producing property?

A. The deduction of depreciation
B. The deduction of interest
C. Capital gains treatment
D. All of the above.

324. Which of the following deeds would contain a granting clause, but carry no warranties, expressed or implied?

A. A deed of trust
B. A trustee's deed
C. A grant deed
D. A quitclaim deed

325. Walters, after signing a contract to purchase real property, but before being notified of the seller's acceptance of the offer, dies of a heart attack. Which of the following is true?

A. Notification to the administrator of the estate would bind Walter's estate.
B. The death of Walters worked a revocation of the offer.
C. The offer and unqualified acceptance constitute an enforceable contract.
D. The sale would not be binding because the deed was not delivered prior to Walter's death.

326. Which of the following least affects the use of land?

A. Zoning ordinances
B. Easements
C. Liens
D. Covenants, conditions and restrictions

327. Every sales contract relating to the purchase of real property in a common interest subdivision or a new subdivision in an unincorporated county area shall clearly set forth

A. the name of the broker.
B. the amount of commission.
C. all outstanding encumbrances.
D. an informal description of the property.

328. "Megalopolis" is an important new term that has been added to the vocabulary of persons working in real estate. The term involves the formation of:

A. Roads
B. Cities
C. Subdivisions
D. Shopping centers

329. A post-dated check

A. Is the same as a check with regard to representation by the maker that the maker has money in the bank to cover it and that maker's failure to have such money may be a crime.
B. Is the equivalent of a promissory note.
C. Cannot justifiably be accepted by a real estate broker as a deposit unless there is full disclosure to the seller.
D. B and C are correct.

330. Your client's petition for a variance has been turned down by the Planning Commission. You should advise him to appeal to

A. the District Court.
B. the Superior Court.
C. the City Council (if in a city), or the Board of Supervisors (if in unincorporated areas).
D. he has no right of appeal.

331. Warranty Deeds are common in other parts of the country, but rarely used in California because

A. damages under a grant deed are more liberal than under a warranty deed.
B. title insurance, with its recourse of the insured against the title company, has largely supplanted the warranty deed with its recourse against the grantor.
C. the Grant Deed, with its two implied covenants, was statutorily created to take the place of the warranty deed.
D. the law favors the use of the grant deed because the implied covenants run with the land, while all other covenants of the warranty deed are personal to the grantee.

332. Space available to meet public demand expands and contracts when stimulated primarily by the fluctuation of

A. turnover of residents.
B. elasticity of demand.
C. interest rates.
D. prices and rents.

333. A homeowner can deduct a portion of which of the following as an expense for income tax purposes?

A. Remodeling
B. Painting a bedroom
C. Depreciation
D. Interest on the home loan

334. Smith owns a single-family residence in which he resides. He trades with Brown for another residence, which Brown is renting to a tenant. Both parties intend to use their newly acquired properties for rental income. Which of the following is true?

A. Smith can negotiate a tax-free exchange.
B. Brown can negotiate a tax-free exchange.
C. Both parties can negotiate a tax-free exchange.
D. Neither can negotiate a tax-free exchange.

335. Which of the following normally deals directly with borrowers, underwrites loans, arranges for real property appraisals, and services loans by receiving and crediting monthly payments?

A. Investors who buy GNMA participation certificates.
B. Secondary mortgage market participants.
C. Primary mortgage lenders.
D. Purchasers of real property securities.

336. The form of real estate syndicate that requires 100 or more investors is a

A. corporation.
B. general partnership.
C. limited partnership.
D. Real Estate Investment Trust (REIT).

337. When a lender accepts a deed in lieu of foreclosure, the lender

A. must also have the power of sale.
B. must take ownership of property free and clear of all liens.
C. must go to court and get deficiency judgment.
D. assumes junior loans.

338. The words "Time is of the essence" would most likely be found in a

A. bill of sale.
B. trust deed.
C. listing.
D. deposit receipt.

339. Interest calculated on the total sum of the principal and the simple interest accrued thereon is called

A. simple interest.
B. compound interest.
C. penalty interest.
D. interest rate.

340. It is proper business practice for real property managers to be compensated in all of the following ways except by a

A. percentage of gross receipts.
B. commission on new leases.
C. commission on major repairs or alterations.
D. receipt of discounts on purchase of supplies.

341. Common ownership of a recreation area and individual ownership of individual lots is a/an

A. condominium.
B. planned development project.
C. apartment project.
D. cooperative project.

342. Which term does not belong with the others?

A. Convey
B. Transfer
C. Devise
D. Assign

343. The responsibility of an agent to his principal is to

A. help him spend money on real property.
B. show him real estate on Rodeo Drive.
C. tell him how lucky he are (is) to have you as an agent because you are working for him around the clock.
D. show them the correct fiduciary responsibilities and keep them up-to-date on all the things that you are doing for him.

344. A "beneficiary statement" is often required in the closing of an escrow in the sale of a real property. This is a statement

A. issued by a lender indicating the balance due on a loan.
B. found in an insurance policy designating the recipient of the benefits.
C. made by the seller as to the features of the property.
D. rendered to the broker as to the amount of commission.

345. The personal, revocable and unassignable permission or authority to do one or more acts on the land of another without possessing any interest therein is a definition of a/an

A. license.
B. easement.
C. encumbrance.
D. option.

346. The sheet metal that is used to protect a building from water seepage is called

A. gutter.
B. flashing.
C. sheeting.
D. none of the above.

347. Upon seeking housing accommodations, a person who found himself discriminated against may, under Title VIII of the Civil Rights Act of 1968

A. bring an action in either federal or state court.
B. file criminal charges in state court only.
C. initiate criminal action in federal court only.
D. file civil action in the State Superior Court for specific action only.

348. According to the Bulk Sales Law, when buying a business one must

A. post a Notice of Sale in a public place.
B. notify individual creditors.
C. publish the notification of sale.
D. all of the above.

349. A cost that is most likely overlooked when the owner of a commercial property lists it for the purpose of sale is

A. unsatisfactory floor plan.
B. management costs.
C. deferred maintenance.
D. economic obsolescence.

350. A tract developer learns that a large national cosmetics manufacturer is moving near an area where he is building a large number of new homes/condominiums. Since many of the cosmetic firm's employees are women, he decides to gear his sales promotions toward this group and advertises accordingly. Realizing he can't discriminate towards any one racial group, he has his agents set up a quota for Caucasian, Black, Chicano, and Asian buyers. Once the quota is reached, they should discourage any further sales to the group by readjusting the prices. If the developer follows this plan he violates

A. no fair housing laws.
B. the fair housing laws based on his ad campaign but not the quota system.
C. the fair housing laws based on his racial quota system but not the ad campaign.
D. the fair housing laws in both his ad campaign and racial quota system.

351. A buyer executes a real estate purchase contract and receipt for deposit on January 10 and gives the broker a check for $500. The buyer instructs the broker to hold the check in uncashed form until January 30, regardless of when the offer is accepted. Under these circumstances the broker should

A. deposit the check with escrow the next business day following an acceptance of the offer.
B. refuse to accept the check and offer under these terms.
C. give the check to the seller if the offer is accepted regardless of the date.
D. present the offer but inform the seller that the check is to be held until January 30.

352. Who will establish the real property tax rate?

A. Board of Supervisors
B. Tax Assessor
C. Tax Commissioner
D. Board of Equalization

353. Regarding the California Land Title Association Policy of Title Insurance: which of the following would indicate the advantage of having an extended coverage as opposed to standard coverage?

A Forgery
B. Lack of capacity
C. Government regulations
D. Physical aspects

354. A contract between the seller of real property and a licensee, in which the seller agrees to pay the licensee a commission if he produces a ready, willing, and able buyer and the licensee agrees to use due diligence in procuring the buyer, is called a

A. bilateral executed contract.
B. unilateral executory contract.
C. unilateral executed contract.
D. bilateral executory contract.

355. In a typical percentage lease, rent is calculated as a percentage of

A. assets of the lessee's business.
B. net sales of the lessee's business.
C. gross sales of the lessee's business.
D. net taxable income of the lessee's business.

356. A land developer offers a free prize to anyone who replies to his direct mail advertisement and visits his subdivision site. Prior to awarding the prize however, the developer requires the party to attend a sales presentation at the site. The sales presentation requirement was not mentioned anywhere in the advertisement. This type of promotion is

A. illegal because it did not disclose the sales representation attendance requirement.
B. legal if the prize is actually awarded.
C. illegal because free prizes cannot be offered under any circumstances.
D. legal if the prize winners purchase a property.

357. A restriction in a deed would be enforced by a

A. housing inspector.
B. planning commission.
C. court injunction.
D. Board of Realtors.

358. Which of the following contracts must be in writing to be enforceable?

A. A lease for one year
B. A listing to lease for one year
C. An agreement by a buyer to assume an existing loan secured by a deed of trust
D. An agreement between brokers to share a commission

359. While appraising a home, an appraiser observes cracks in the foundation and notices that the doors and windows do not close properly. The appraiser would probably recommend which of the following?

A. A termite report
B. A soil engineer's report
C. A special studies zone report
D. A home warranty protection policy

360. Edward Sampson and Jerome P. Dickson, single men, wish to take title to real property so that each will own a one-half interest with right of survivorship. The granting clause should read

A. "Edward Sampson, a single man, and Jerome P. Dickson, a single man, each an undivided one-half interest as tenants-in-common."
B. "Edward Sampson, a single man, and Jerome P. Dickson, a single man, as joint tenants."
C. "Edward Sampson and Jerome P. Dickson, unmarried men, each a one-half interest."
D. None of the above is correct.

361. Some leases contain a covenant or condition against assignment without consent of the lessor. In such a case, if the lessee makes an assignment unknown to the lessor, the assignment is considered

A. voidable.
B. a forfeiture.
C. void.
D. a termination.

362. A beneficiary statement is issued by the

A. lender to the borrower to identify current status of a loan.
B. lender to identify who benefits from the loan proceeds.
C. borrower to the lender to verify past income.
D. borrower to the lender for credit purposes.

363. Highest and best use most nearly means

A. greatest net return.
B. greatest gross return.
C. tallest building allowed under local zoning.
D. none of the above.

364. In 2009, an appraiser appraised a house using the cost approach. It was determined that the house, which measured 30 feet by 50 feet, and the garage, which measured 12 feet by 18 feet, were 10 years old. The appraiser estimated that they would have a total economic life of 50 years. In 2009, the cost to construct the house new was $10.20 per square foot, and the cost to construct the garage new was $3.25 per square foot. The value of the land was determined to be $1,500. So in 2009, the depreciated value of the property would be

A. $10,000.
B. $12,500.
C. $14,301.60.
D. $14,824.40.

365. A final value estimate is the correlation, or reconciliation, of the value indications obtained from which of the following approaches?

A. Cost, development, and income
B. Cost, comparative, and market data
C. Cost, income, and comparative
D. Income, land residual, and market data

366. Ron owns a home, which rents for $600 per month. The home across the street rents for $690 per month and recently sold for $78,000. If Ron applies the same gross rent multiplier to his home as was used on the home across the street, what is the approximate value of Ron's home?

A. $50,000
B. $67,800
C. $69,595
D. $70,909

367. When a transaction takes place for the sale of a business, on which of the following would a sales tax be charged?

A. Furniture and/or fixtures
B. Stock-in-trade
C. Goodwill
D. All of the above.

368. Recording a judgment gives what type of notice?

A. Actual notice.
B. Constructive notice.
C. Incomplete notice.
D. Written notice.

369. Because life insurance companies are not willing to deal directly with the mortgagors and trustors, they usually pay a loan servicing and preparation fee, and make real estate mortgage loans to purchase indirectly through

A. Savings and loan associations
B. Mortgage companies
C. FHA or VA
D. Any of the above.

370. A blanket encumbrance is one that

A. was originated to pay off several small trust deeds on a property.
B. constitutes a lien on real property and cannot be partially paid off.
C. covers more than one lot or parcel.
D. gives overall permission to use all or any part of a person's property.

371. When issuing their closing statement, escrow would debit the seller of income property for which of the following items

A. prepaid taxes.
B. prepaid rent.
C. prepaid fire insurance premium.
D. all of the above.

372. Under normal competitive conditions, the vacancy rate of an apartment building is the result of

A. housing supply and demand in the area.
B. employment fluctuations.
C. cost of construction and the cost of money.
D. schedule of rents and number of units in the apartment building.

373. Community apartment projects and condominiums come within the subdivision provisions of the California Real Estate Law when they contain how many units?

A. One or more
B. Five or more
C. Three or more
D. Two or more

374. Broker Wilson is asked by Mr. Able to assist him in obtaining a $1,500 loan secured by a trust deed on his unimproved property. Broker Wilson secured a 90-day exclusive listing on the loan from Mr. Able. In regards to this transaction,

A. a listing for a loan of $2,000 or less is limited to a term of not more than 45 days.
B. Broker Wilson cannot arrange a loan on unimproved property.
C. Broker Wilson must have a real property securities dealer's license.
D. Broker Wilson has done nothing wrong.

375. A broker who holds a valid listing on a property places a classifieds ad for the property containing only the following information: "For Sale 3 bedroom, 2 bath home with swimming pool. Asking Price $149,000. Telephone 281-5211." This type of advertisement would be an example of a

A. display ad.
B. blind ad.
C. qualified ad.
D. silent ad.

376. Which of the following would not be classified as an institutional lender?

A. Insurance company.
B. Mortgage company.
C. Savings and loan association.
D. Commercial bank.

377. After signing a valid agreement for sale, a buyer asks the broker for permission to move into the property before the sale closes. The broker should

A. have the buyer sign a temporary lease on the property.
B. give the buyer oral permission.
C. deny the buyer permission.
D. obtain written consent from the seller.

378. If a buyer withdraws his offer to purchase real property prior to acceptance by the seller, the

A. buyer is entitled to a refund of the earnest money deposit.
B. Seller may sue the buyer for specific performance and will probably win the sit.
C. broker may sue the buyer for specific performance.
D. seller is entitled to one-half of the earnest money deposit.

379. Regarding a Trust Deed and Note, the

A. Trust Deed outlaws before the Note.
B. provisions of the Trust Deed will prevail if there is a conflict between these and the provisions of the Note concerning the maturity of the debt.
C. note is less important that the Trust Deed.
D. lien of the Trust Deed is incidental to the debt.

380. An institutional lender would be LEAST interested in which of the following?

A. Value of the property
B. Borrower's income
C. Amount of down payment
D. Borrower's desire for the property

381. An offer made by the buyer was accepted by the seller. Prior to the broker advising the buyer that the offer had been accepted, the buyer died. The contract would be

A. void.
B. voidable.
C. valid and binding on the executor of the estate.
D. valid and binding on the broker.

382. A significant difference between Mechanics liens and Judgment liens is that

A. mechanics liens are created by statute.
B. judgment liens are not enforceable until recorded.
C. judgment liens are involuntary.
D. mechanics liens may take priority earlier than the date they are recorded.

383. The provision that states "The Realtor shall not publicly disparage the business practice of a competitor" appears in the

A. Real Estate Law.
B. Commissioner's Rules and Regulations.
C. NAR Code of Ethics.
D. Business and Professions Code.

384. Which of the following types of lenders would have the greatest percentage of, and the most funds invested in, real estate mortgages?

A. Credit unions.
B. Commercial banks.
C. Life insurance companies.
D. Mutual savings banks.

385. Which of the following items would most likely appear as a credit on the sellers' closing statement?

A. Prepaid taxes
B. An assumed loan
C. Title insurance premium
D. Delinquent assessment lien

386. The primary purpose of zoning ordinances is to:

A. promote conformity in the outward appearances of structures.
B. limit the supply of specific businesses within a zoned area.
C. promote the general health, safety, and welfare of the community.
D. increase the tax base of the local governing body.

387. Mrs. Adams dies intestate and apparently has no heirs. She has substantial property holdings in California, therefore the

A. property would be sold for back property taxes if no heirs would claim the property within five years.
B. property would escheat to the State of California if no heirs should claim the property within five years.
C. trustee would dictate the disposition of the estate.
D. city would dictate the disposition of the estate should no heirs be found.

388. Which of the following is used in determining the net income of a property using the Capitalization Approach of appraisal?

A. Reserves for depreciation
B. Income tax paid
C. Vacancy allowance
D. Payments on a mortgage loan

389. The county tax rate is set annually by the

A. Board of Supervisors.
B. County Treasurer.
C. County Assessor.
D. State Board of Equalization.

390. In regard to land value units, as the depth a lot increases beyond the typical lot depth, the

A. front foot value and square foot unit value both decrease.
B. square foot unit value increases.
C. value of the lot decreases.
D. value per front foot increases.

391. From an historical standpoint, the major function, objective, and aim of the Federal Housing Administration program has been provided by which of the following sections of law?

A. Title I
B. Title II
C. Title III
D. Title IV

392. The total value of all goods and services produced by the U.S. during a specific period of time is called the

A. Federal Reserve.
B. Composite Index.
C. Gross Domestic Budget.
D. Gross National Product (GNP).

393. The area between the bottom of the floor joists and the ground is called a crawl space. According to FHA minimum property requirements, it must be at least

A. 12 inches.
B. 16 inches.

C. 18 inches.
D. 24 inches.

394. An easement that could be most easily terminated by non-use would be created by which method?

A. A quitclaim deed from a valid owner
B. Express reservation in a deed
C. Prescription
D. Implication

395. Which of the following agencies is primarily concerned with affordable rental housing?

A. Federal Housing Administration (FHA)
B. Urban Renewal Development (URD)
C. Veterans Administration (VA)
D. Department of Housing and Urban Development (HUD)

396. Which of the following would describe a change in flight patterns of airplanes that would make them fly over an owner's property?

A. Economic obsolescence
B. Functional obsolescence
C. Deterioration
D. Any of the above.

397. In California, a Grant Deed normally transfers title of real property to the:

A. owner.
B. seller.
C. beneficiary.
D. grantee.

398. In the event of a business failure, a limited partner may limit his or her liability to outside creditors to

A. all liabilities of the partnership.
B. the secured liabilities of the partnership.
C. the total amount of his or her pledged contribution to the partnership.
D. none of the liabilities of the partnership.

399. The best appraisal methods to be used to establish the current market value of a shopping center would be the

A. Replacement Cost - Income (capitalization).
B. Market Data - Income (capitalization).
C. Income (capitalization) - Gross rent multiplier.
D. Replacement Cost - Gross rent multiplier.

400. The four elements of production are Labor, Capital, Entrepreneurship, and

A. Dedication.
B. Skill.
C. Land.
D. Profit.

401. In doing the Reproduction Cost approach to appraising, taking the cost of each individual item into account to come up with accurate figures describes which method?

A. Unit in place method
B. Square foot method
C. Quantity survey method
D. Cubic foot method

402. Two friends hold title to a home as joint tenants. One of them borrowed money and executed a note and a deed of trust against the home. This action could

A. destroy one of the four unities of the joint tenancy.
B. place the beneficiary in a precarious position should the borrower die before the debt is paid.
C. invalidate the note since a lien can attach only to the undivided interest of all joint tenants.
D. create a security interest in all other real property in which the borrower may have an interest.

403. "No person acting under the Real Estate Law shall accept any purchase or loan funds or other consideration from a prospective purchaser or lender, or directly or indirectly cause such funds or other consideration to be deposited to an escrow except as to the specific loan or specific real property sales contract or promissory note secured directly or collaterally by a lien on real property on which loan, contract or note the person has a bonafide authorization to negotiate or to sell." In the preceding quotation taken from the Real Estate Law, the term "collaterally" means a

A. hard money note.
B. note secured by another note.
C. purchase money loan.
D. real property security.

404. There are many advantages in purchasing a home using government insured or guaranteed loans. Some of these advantages include lower down payments, lower interest rates, and a longer term to pay off the loan. Which of the following statement is NOT true with regard to these loans?

A. FHA loans can be made on property that is to be owner-occupied or rented to others.
B. VA loans are made on single-family homes where the borrower intends to rent to others.
C. Cal-Vet buyers cannot rent their homes to others unless they have received prior permission from the Department of Veterans Affairs.
D. Qualified veterans who served in Viet Nam are eligible for Cal-Vet or GI loans.

405. The use of the "gross multiplier" to assist in appraising real property leased to various tenants is based upon

A. gross income in relation to capitalized value.
B. relationship between rental value and sales price, or market value, of property.
C. gross income and anticipated gross income.
D. scheduled gross income and expected net income.

406. A Gift Deed conveying title to real property may be set aside or voided by

A. creditors of the grantor.
B. debtor of the grantor.
C. someone who later purchases the land from the Gift Deed grantor.
D. no one.

407. The relationship of principal and agent can be created in all of these ways, EXCEPT by

A. express contract.
B. oral agreement.
C. ratification.
D. subornation.

408. Which of the following types of loans may have a variable amortization period?

A. Cal-Vet
B. FHA
C. VA
D. Any of the above

409. A broker who holds an option on real property and who intends to sell the property to another after exercising the option, should inform the purchaser that the broker is acting as

A. An optionor.
B. A beneficiary.
C. A mortgagor.
D. A principal.

410. Which of the following is not a secondary mortgage market lender?

A. Federal Housing Administration (FHA)
B. Federal National Mortgage Association (Fannie Mae)
C. Government National Mortgage Association (Ginnie Mae)
D. Federal Home Loan Mortgage Corporation (Freddie Mac)

411. A homeowner can deduct all of the following costs for his primary residence each year on his federal tax return, except

A. an uninsured casualty loss.
B. local real property taxes.
C. painting the living room.
D. the portion of his monthly mortgage payment attributable to the payment of interest.

412. After Mr. Bagger purchased his home, he discovered by survey that his neighbor's garage was three feet over on his newly acquired property. This disturbed him greatly. For remedy, if a friendly settlement cannot be reached, he should bring civil suit against

A. the broker, for failure to disclose the encroachment.
B. his neighbor.
C. the Real Estate Commissioner.
D. the title company, for failure to show the encumbrance on the standard form title report.

413. A Prepaid Rental Listing Agent is required to do all of the following, EXCEPT

A. give a contract and receipt to every prospective tenant, which provides for return of the fee under certain conditions.
B. repay any amount over $25 if a rental is not obtained.
C. return the entire fee if no referrals are received within five days of the execution of the agreement.
D. submit a statement of accounts to the Commissioner quarterly.

414. Gary buys a home from Lee, paying all cash. Lee still owed money against the property. If everything is done correctly, what would most likely be recorded?

A. Deed of Reconveyance to Gary
B. Deed of Reconveyance to Lee
C. Trust Deed against Gary
D. Bill of Sale

415. Which of the following would best describe deferred maintenance?

A. An apartment building with no air conditioning.
B. A building needing an elevator.
C. A building showing signs of needing rehabilitation.
D. A building just newly painted.

416. A roof with slopes on all four sides is called a

A. gambrel roof.
B. gable roof.
C. hip roof.
D. flat roof.

417. In negotiating certain loans a broker is required to fill in all of the items on a Broker's Loan Statement form. Which of the following must be inserted?

A. What the borrower intends to do with the proceeds of the loan, less expenses.
B. A statement of the value of the property supported by a proper appraisal.
C. The date on which the borrower acquired the property.
D. The amount that will be charged by a qualified agency to render a report on the financial capacity of the borrower.

418. To impose restrictions on a new large subdivision, the most practical method is to

A. record the restrictions in the manner provided by law and make reference to them in each deed.
B. publish the restrictions in a newspaper of general circulation.
C. post the restrictions on the property.
D. include the restrictions as covenants in all the deeds.

419. A broker receives an offer on a property, and a prospective purchaser gives him a $1,000 deposit. He places the deposit in his trust account. After all the conditions of the deposit receipt have been fulfilled, the buyer decides that he wants to back out. The seller agrees to release the buyer if he may keep $500 of the deposit money. However, the buyer claims that he "has an out" because of a certain clause in the deposit receipt and demands the return of the entire $1,000. The seller then demands the $1,000 from the broker. The broker should

A. give the $1,000 to the seller.
B. give the $1,000 to the buyer.
C. keep the $1,000 in his trust account.
D. none of the above.

420. The Hutchinsons, prospective buyers of a home, request a broker to find a loan for them. The broker would most likely contact

A. an institutional lender, such as a bank, or a savings and loan association.
B. a Federal Reserve Bank.
C. the Federal Housing Administration.
D. an FHA appraiser.

421. Which of the following principles of value forms the basis of the Market Data approach? The principle of

A. Substitution
B. Anticipation
C. Change
D. Conformity

422. A high Energy Efficiency Ratio (EER) on an air conditioning unit means

A. the unit is more efficient.
B. the unit is less efficient.

C. the unit needs more electricity per BTU produced.
D. air conditioners do not use energy efficiency ratios.

423. In certain types of real estate transactions, the term "like for like" is used. What type of transaction would this most likely be?

A. An assessment of property
B. A market comparison appraisal
C. A tax-free exchange
D. A residential sale

424. Which of the following is not an essential to acquiring an Easement by Prescription?

A. Open and Notorious
B. Hostile to the owner
C. Payment of the real property taxes
D. Claim of right/color of title

425. When estimating the loss in value due to depreciation, the real estate appraiser would primarily be concerned with

A. economic life.
B. actual age.
C. Chronological age.
D. remaining life.

426. The personal, revocable, and unassignable permission to authority to do one or more acts on the land of another without possessing any interest thereon, is a definition of:

A. A license
B. An easement
C. An encumbrance
D. An option

427. A salesperson receives an offer from a buyer who has no cash but offers a deposit of $500 in the form of a personal note payable in thirty days. Which statement is true?

A. This is unacceptable since a deposit must be in cash or check.
B. The form of deposit is immaterial as long as the $500 figure appears on the deposit receipt.
C. A salesperson may accept a personal note as deposit if he advises the seller of this prior to acceptance and receives the seller's permission to accept the deposit.
D. A salesperson may accept a note if made in favor of the broker to handle expenses.

428. A prudent lender would take into consideration which of the following before issuing a loan?

A. Borrower's ability to pay
B. The market value of property that is the security for the loan
C. Current economic trends
D. All of the above.

429. In assessing the profitability of a real estate office, the broker must consider "desk cost." Which best describes how to calculate "desk cost"?

A. Calculate the cost of all the desks.
B. Calculate the gross profit for the office, less the expenses, divide by the number of desks.
C. Divide the total cost of rent, utilities, and advertising by the number of desks.
D. Divide the total operating expenses of the office, including salaries, rent, insurance, etc., by the number of desks.

430. The economic life of an improvement as compared to the physical life is usually

A. longer.
B. shorter.
C. the same.
D. it depends on the type of improvement.

431. A private party offers a single family residence for sale without the services of a real estate broker and advertises that the property is to be sold in an "as is" condition. Under these circumstances the seller

A. need not disclose any known defects in the property.
B. must provide a Real Estate Transfer Disclosure Statement to a prospective buyer.
C. need not provide a Real Estate Transfer Disclosure Statement to a prospective buyer.
D. has invoked the "Caveat Emptor" (Buyer Beware) representation and has no further obligation to a prospective buyer.

432. Which of the following is real property?

A. Stock in a mutual water company
B. Fruit on trees already sold by contract
C. Minerals or gas removed from the ground
D. Crops before harvest

433. Mike Coogan, a new real estate salesperson, made strong efforts to obtain listings in a non-integrated community. He found success by insinuating to property owners that should minorities move into the area, the value of their homes would decrease. Which of the following terms best describes the activities of salesperson Coogan?

A. Steering
B. Panic Selling
C. Blockbusting
D. Both B and C.

434. Harris and Davis, single people, owned a parcel of real property as joint tenants. Harris encumbered his interest for $10,000, borrowing the amount to pay medical bills without the knowledge or consent of Davis. Shortly thereafter, Harris died with the debt still unpaid. Which of the following would be true?

A. Davis and the lender would be tenants in common, each owning one half interest in the property.
B. Davis would own all of the property free and clear of the encumbrance.
C. Davis would own all of the property, but would be subject to the $10,000 loan.
D. Davis and the beneficiary would own the property as joint tenants, each with a one-half interest.

435. A builder purchased a tract of land, convincing the seller to finance part of the purchase price with a note and deed of trust, which contained a subordination clause. That clause could:

A. Create additional liens against the property without the consent of the buyer.
B. Result in future liens placed on the property by the buyer to have priority.

C. Ensure that the first trust deed always has priority over all other loans.
D. Render invalid any construction loan placed against the property.

436. What supports the floor and ceiling loads?

A. Joists
B. Studs
C. Supporters
D. Mud sills

437. A broker who takes a listing with option to purchase is, first of all a/an

A. principal.
B. optionor.
C. optionee.
D. agent.

438. Mr. and Mrs. Davis held real property as "husband and wife." Mr. Davis died and his will specified that "all his interests" were to go to his eldest son, Thomas. Son Thomas would

A. Inherit an undivided one-half interest in the property.
B. Acquire a one-half interest with his mother as joint tenant.
C. Acquire title to the property in Fee Simple, as he is the eldest male heir.
D. Acquire no interest in the property as it would automatically go to the widow.

439. The Real Estate Commissioner's Final Subdivision Public Report expires

A. one year from date of report.
B. never, unless a material change occurs.
C. five years from date of issuance of report.
D. when four or less lots remain to be sold.

440. An individual purchased a nine-acre parcel of unimproved property. He then subdivided the nine acres into one-acre parcels. If the subdivider plans to sell only three 1-acre parcels per year over the next three years, he must comply with

A. the State Subdivision Map Act.
B. the State Subdivided Lands Act.
C. both A and B above.
D. neither A or B above.

441. In advertising a listed property for sale, a broker may not legally

A. run an ad that does not give the listing price of the property.
B. state the kind of financing available.
C. fail to state the street address of the property.
D. run an ad giving the impression that he is the owner of the property.

442. An appraiser, in arriving at an estimate of value secured under each of the three approaches in appraising

A. averages the estimates.
B. assigns weights to the estimates and then averages them.
C. chooses the approach the appraiser judges as best and uses that approach alone.
D. explains why or why not the other approaches were not used, then chooses the one the appraiser believes to be the most appropriate approach.

443. A licensed contractor purchased eight lots in a new subdivision and constructed eight homes on the lots. He sold the eight homes to various buyers and took back a $5,000 Second Trust Deed on each of them. He would now like to sell the Trust Deeds within the year of their creation at a 20% discount. In order for him to do this, he

A. needs a real estate brokers' license.
B. must sell them through a Real Property Securities Dealer.
C. does not need a permit.
D. must deliver a Real Property Security Statement.

444. The owner of a property who signed a listing with a broker for 30 days was killed in an accident before the listing expired. The listing is

A. no good as an authorization, but binding if a buyer is secured later.
B. still in effect as the owner's interest was clear.
C. binding upon owner's heirs to carry out his promises.
D. terminated by the death of the owner.

445. Which of the following would usually be considered real property?

A. Cut timber
B. Air space above the land
C. Unharvested crops that have already been contracted
D. Land fill dirt being moved

446. A Veteran's Exemption must be filed by

A. March 15.
B. April 15.
C. May 15.
D. June 15.

447. When compared to a conventional contract of sale, the distinguishing characteristic of a real estate option is its

A. irrevocability.
B. mutuality of contract.
C. lack of mutuality in obligation.
D. both B and C.

448. The Real Estate Commissioner would be prevented from proceeding with a formal action against the license of a real estate broker by the

A. closing of the broker's office.
B. broker moving to another state.
C. lapse of three years from the occurrence of the grounds of complaint.
D. expiration of the broker's license.

449. A minority purchaser enters your office and states they are looking for, and interested in purchasing, a particular property in a minority neighborhood. You could legally assume that

A. this person is testing you.
B. they are interested in that particular property.
C. they are interested in owning a home in an all minority neighborhood.
D. they cannot qualify to own property in a higher priced area.

450. Certain charges are prohibited by the Real Estate Settlement Procedures Act in selling a house. Buyer or seller may legally be charged for all of the following EXCEPT

A. disclosure settlement statements.
B. credit reports.
C. appraisals necessary to make the loan.
D. preparation of loan documents.

451. Concerning business opportunities

A. the Bulk Sales Law is contained in the Uniform Commercial Code.
B. a Bill of Sale is used to convey title to business items.
C. sales Tax is a tax on the sale of tangible personal property.
D. all of the above.

452. The primary justification for zoning ordinances is to

A. maintain conformity to buildings in the zoned area.
B. prevent an oversupply of certain types of businesses.
C. promote the public health, safety, morals and general welfare.
D. control the quality of building construction.

453. An attorney drew up a contract between a buyer and a seller for the purchase of a property. The agreement included a liquidated damages clause calling for the payment of $500 in the event the buyer should default. Prior to the close of escrow, the buyer decided that the home would not suit her family and canceled the purchase. If the seller were to sue for specific performance, he would most likely be

A. successful because the $500 is not adequate considering the value of the property.
B. successful because the reason for canceling by the buyer was not strong.
C. unsuccessful because the seller agreed to accept the $500 as liquidated damages in the contract.
D. unsuccessful because an attorney drew the contract.

454. The right to foreclose on a trust deed, under a trustee's power of sale, outlaws

A. in four years.
B. in three years.
C. in two years.
D. never.

455. Option to renew a lease is a

A. covenant.
B. restriction.
C. limitation.
D. condition.

456. RESPA requires delivery of the Uniform Settlement Statement no later than

A. 10 calendar days after the loan commitment is made.
B. 3 business days prior to the close of the transaction.
C. 1 calendar day prior to the close of the transaction.
D. At or before the date of settlement.

457. The owner of a single-family residence plans to sell, and wants to obtain an FHA appraisal to permit a sale with FHA financing. He should

A. contact the nearest FHA office for an appraisal of this property.
B. have a lender apply for a firm commitment.
C. have a lender apply for a conditional commitment.
D. submit a recent appraisal of his home to FHA.

458. Which of the following is the classic definition of the boundaries of real property?

A. The surface area indicated on a map
B. A reasonable use of airspace and extended to the center of the earth
C. A reasonable distance down and unlimited airspace
D. A practical or reasonable use of the earth and unlimited airspace

459. When the sale of a business also involves the bulk sale of the stock, a notice of the sale must be given as provided in the

A. California Real Estate Law.
B. California Civil Code.
C. Uniform Commercial Code.
D. Article 7 of the Business and Professions Code.

460. Should a person be discriminated against, what would best describe the actions available to them?

A. Private action in a state or federal court
B. Civil action in State Superior Court
C. Criminal action in a state court
D. Criminal action in a federal court

461. A lessee's interest is

A. personal property.
B. a Chattel Real.
C. a grant to use property for a period of time that reverts to the grantor at the expiration of the term.
D. all of the above.

462. A licensed real estate broker received a signed listing from a prospective seller. During the listed period, the broker found a buyer who submitted an offer that was $1,000 less than the listed price. The owner accepted the offer as submitted and the buyer was notified of the acceptance. After escrow was opened, buyer and seller agreed to cancel the sale but the seller refused to pay the broker a commission. Under the Statute of Limitations how long does the broker have to sue for his commission?

A. Ninety days
B. One year
C. Two years
D. Four years

463. In the state of California, which department or board receives the Structural Pest Control Reports?

A. The Department of Real Estate
B. The Bureau of Entomology
C. The Structural Pest Control Board
D. None of the above. It remains with the city or county where the inspection took place.

464. The one unity in a joint tenancy holding that is also present in tenancy-in-common holding is

A. equal right of possession.
B. right of survivorship.
C. equal interest of all owners.
D. tenants in possession can be charged rent for the use of the land.

465. Capitalization is an appraisal process used to

A. convert net income into market value.
B. establish book value.
C. determine net income.
D. establish a capitalization rate.

466. An employee of a corporation licensed as a real estate broker that is working as a member of the corporation's sales staff

A. does not require a real estate salesperson's license.
B. must be a licensed real estate broker.
C. must be a licensed real estate salesperson or broker.
D. does not require a real estate license provided that person is an officer of the corporation.

467. Which of the following, when authorized by the broker, could make a withdrawal from the broker's trust account?

A. No one can ever withdraw money from the broker's trust account except the broker himself.
B. Any employee, as long as the broker is incorporated
C. Any employee provided that the employee is covered by a surety bond protecting the broker
D. Any of the broker's licensees

468. Concerning Riparian Rights, which of the following is true?

A. Give absolute ownership of adjacent waters.
B. Are set forth in a standard title insurance policy.
C. Include the right to reasonably appropriate water as needed.
D. May accurately be determined from an examination of public records.

469. To use the Capitalization Approach to appraising you need the

A. gross income only.
B. occupations of the tenants.
C. net income.
D. cash flow.

470. In the event a court proceeding is entered into between two licensed real estate brokers over a commission split, it is not necessary for the brokers to show the court a written contract between the brokers regarding the commission split because

A. this type of agreement is not covered under the Statute of Frauds.
B. it is judicial recognition that this is a common practice between cooperating brokers.
C. the Real Estate Law specifically exempts these contracts.
D. no Listing Agreement or Commission Agreement needs to be in writing to be enforceable in court.

471. Which of the following is not required to obtain an easement by prescription:

A. A use of the property hostile and adverse to the true owner's title.
B. A public confrontation with the owner before witnesses.
C. A claim of right.
D. Open, notorious, and uninterrupted use for five years.

472. An escrow officer received two pest control reports that had been prepared by two different licensed structural pest control operators and based on their separate inspections. If the report was part of the terms of the purchase agreement and one recommended more corrective work than the other, the escrow officer should

A. have the seller select which report to furnish the buyer.
B. select the one with the greater amount of recommended corrective work and give the seller and buyer a copy.
C. send a copy of both reports to both the seller and the buyer.
D. send a copy of both reports to the broker and let the broker decide which report should be released.

473. In order to secure an FHA home loan, a new buyer would normally do all of the following except:

A. Find a lender who will be willing to grant him the loan.
B. Apply to the nearest office of the FHA for an appraisal.
C. Agree to pay for mortgage insurance protection.
D. Buy a home which meets the FHA requirements and restrictions.

474. Fisk owns a lot. He also owns a right-of-way easement over the property of his neighbor, Smith. This easement is appurtenant to Fisk's lot. Fisk sells his lot to Jones without specific mention of the easement in the deed. The easement

A. remains with Fisk as an encumbered interest.
B. passes to Jones.
C. terminates unless it is a covenant running with the land.
D. reverts to Smith.

475. Which of the following would normally install conduit?

A. Plumbers
B. Electricians
C. Roofers
D. Carpenters

476. Two people entered into a land contract for the purchase of a home and the contract was recorded. A few months later, the vendee abandons the property and defaults on the contract. If the vendee refuses to execute and record some form of release, it will

A. not affect the marketability of the property.
B. result in a deficiency judgment.
C. result in a trustee's sale.
D. create a cloud on the title.

477. A broker who is hired by an owner to sell his property must reveal all significant and material information to the principal. Which of the following would be considered material information and must be revealed?

A. The new lender will require the buyer to maintain an impound account.
B. Agent's knowledge that a better offer to purchase is imminent.
C. The prospective buyer is of Asian descent.
D. None of the above.

478. Generally, the most important determinant of a property's value is

A. age.
B. utility.
C. location.
D. income.

479. Real property includes the land, those things attached to the land, and things called appurtenances. Appurtenances include all of the following except

A. a dwelling.
B. trade fixtures.
C. watercourses.
D. a fence.

480. The cost approach used on a residence built in 1912 would require

A. determination of labor costs in 1912.
B. labor costs in 1912 to be adjusted by an index.
C. average labor costs over the period.
D. replacement cost determined by today's costs less depreciation.

481. Mr. O'Riley paid an owner $10 for an option containing this clause: "Option to be for 60 days from June 1, 2012. Upon exercise of option, holder is to purchase within 30 days thereafter for all cash consideration." On July 10, Mr. O'Riley sold and assigned his option for $1,000. On July 28, the new holder notified the owner that he would purchase on August 15. The owner claimed the option was void. The option was

A. void, because the holder sold it.
B. void, because date of purchase was not within the option period.
C. valid, even though Mr. O'Riley sold it, but August 15 was too late for date of sale.
D. valid, and assignee could purchase on August 15.

482. The appraiser has been employed to appraise a property zoned R-1. Which of the following factors would be considered to be the most important?

A. Zoning
B. Neighborhood sites
C. Marketability and acceptability
D. Adjoining property owners of the same economic level

483. For the contract or agreement to be enforceable, a person signing under a "Power of Attorney" should sign

A. principal's name only to the agreement.
B. their name only to the agreement.
C. their and their principal's name to the agreement.
D. in any of the above manners.

484. A house sold for $345,000, which was 9% more than the cost of the house. The original cost of the house was most nearly

A. $300,300.
B. $306,500.
C. $310,150.
D. $316,500.

485. When would a lender look to a borrower's personal assets? When the borrower was

A. a corporation.
B. a partnership (general).
C. a limited partnership.
D. none of the above.

486. A husband who owns separate property dies without a will. Concerning that separate property, it would be distributed in which of the following ways?

A. One-half to the wife and one-half to the children.
B. One-third to the wife and two-thirds to the children if there is more than one child.
C. It would escheat to the state.
D. It would be divided equally among his heirs.

487. When a Special Assessment Tax is imposed under the Street Improvement Act of 1911, property owners are charged with a share of the costs of the new improvement. If the bill is not paid within 30 days of receipt it becomes a lien and

A. the city can foreclose the property immediately.
B. the full amount of the lien is billed on the next bill.
C. it automatically goes to bond and is payable over a period of years.
D. the contractor involved has another 30 days to file a mechanic's lien.

488. Fee schedules setting forth charges for title policies and other services performed by title companies are set by

A. the Department of Insurance.
B. title insurance companies.
C. the Department of Real Estate.
D. the Department of Corporations.

489. If a seller accepted an offer within a seven-day time limit set out in the contract, but changed the date of possession and initialed the change, which of following would be true?

A. The buyer would be bound by the contract and unable to withdraw his offer.
B. The offer would become a counter-offer and if buyer did not accept, he would lose his deposit.
C. The offer would become a counter-offer, subject to acceptance by buyer.
D. None of the above.

490. Which of the following would be the greatest distance?

A. 1/4 mile
B. 1,320 feet
C. 1 side of 1/4 of 1/4 of Section 16
D. All are the same.

491. The buyer advised the escrow company that he was unable to secure a new First Trust Deed loan. If there was a specific contingency clause concerning this point in the escrow instructions,

A. the buyer could demand the return of his deposit.
B. the escrow officer should close escrow and give the deposit to the seller.
C. the broker could sue for his commission.
D. escrow should be extended another 30 days to enable the buyer to secure other financing.

492. Mrs. Barker sells a $5,000 note secured by a deed of trust to investor Johnson for $3,000. This could be best described as

A. leveraging.
B. discounting.
C. illegal.
D. usurious.

493. If all things are equal, the cost to construct a two-story dwelling with the same square footage would be

A. more than the cost of construction of a one-story dwelling.
B. less than the cost of construction of a one-story dwelling.
C. the same as the cost of construction of a one-story dwelling.
D. none of the above.

494. When the State has given permission to a nonriparian owner of a farm to use a nearby lake, the owner has received this right by

A. Appropriation.
B. Percolation.
C. Eminent Domain.
D. Estoppel.

495. Real property of the estate of a person who died intestate is to be sold by the Administrator. This property can only be sold

A. at public auction.
B. to the highest bidder resulting from a newspaper advertisement.
C. after the Court has approved the terms of sale and the price.
D. for all cash.

496. The doctrine of Escheat most nearly refers to the legal process that is used to

A. legally enforce the partition of real estate.
B. legally enforce the taking of private property for public use.
C. distribute the assets of the estate of a deceased person.
D. cause title to certain real estate to revert to the state.

497. Which of the following is the most commonly used title insurance coverage?

A. American Land Title Association.
B. California Land Title Association Extended Coverage.
C. California Land Title Association Standard Coverage.
D. All are used equally.

498. Real estate loans that are governed by an index that tends to fluctuate during the term of the loan are called

A. conventional loans.
B. ARM loans.
C. carry back loans.
D. PAM loans.

499. An offer to sell a franchise in California must be registered with the Department of Corporations unless it is exempted because the franchiser

A. has a net worth of not less than five million dollars.
B. has a net worth of not less than one million dollars.
C. is a subsidiary of a corporation having a net worth of not less than one million dollars.
D. is incorporated in another state.

500. When appraising a 15-year-old, single-family, owner-occupied home, which of the following factors normally would be given the greatest consideration?

A. The tax assessor's records
B. Replacement costs of the dwelling house plus the cost of the land
C. The capitalization of typical rental properties in the neighborhood
D. The current price paid for other homes in the neighborhood

501. Broker Gross is showing property that he has listed to Lavine. Broker Gross knows that there are massive plumbing repairs to be made. Broker Gross

A. doesn't have to tell the buyer, unless the buyer asks.
B. has to tell the buyer, because he must disclose all material facts.
C. does not have to tell the buyer if the property is sold "as is."
D. none of the above.

502. A real estate broker was in the process of taking a listing from an owner, when during the conversation the owner informed the broker that he did not wish to have his property shown to anyone of a minority background. Under these circumstances, the broker should

A. advise the owner to sell the property himself.
B. advise the owner to list it with another broker.
C. refuse to take the listing.
D. take the listing, as someone else will if he does not.

503. As a general rule concerning land value units, it is recognized that as the depth of a lot increases beyond the typical lot depth the

A. value per front foot increases.
B. square foot unit value increases.
C. value of the lot decreases.
D. front foot value and the square foot unit value decreases.

504. The conscious charging by a private lender of more than the maximum amount of interest allowed by law is known as

A. penury.
B. leverage.
C. usury.
D. assemblage.

505. Which of the following would be appurtenant to the land?

A. Anything acquired by legal right that is to be used with the land for its benefit
B. A right of way over another owner's adjoining land
C. Stock in a mutual water company
D. All of the above.

506. Enacted laws to govern the protection of the people concerning, "health, welfare and safety" are established through

A. Eminent Domain.
B. police power.
C. Board of Equalization.
D. two-thirds majority vote of the people.

507. As "Head of the Family," a husband signed a Declaration of Homestead on the family residence, which was encumbered only by a $92,000 First Trust Deed. The wife did not sign the declaration. The property was worth $108,000. The owner had a new roof put on the house, but did not pay the roofing contractor, who then filed a Mechanics Lien. The lien was

A. not enforceable because homestead property is protected from any liens.
B. enforceable because wife did not sign the Declaration of Homestead.
C. enforceable because Mechanic's Liens take priority over a recorded homestead exemption.
D. not enforceable because with a first trust deed of $92,000 there is no equity above the homestead exemption.

508. The main benefit for the lender under FHA financing over conventional financing is the

A. mortgage insurance.
B. higher yield.
C. ease of sale in the secondary money market.
D. higher loan to value ratio.

509. Rezoning often involves ridding the area of nonconforming use. The means utilized may involve all of the following, except:

A. Prohibition against rebuilding.
B. Prohibition against extending.
C. Retroactive zoning ordinances.
D. Amortization provisions terminating use within a reasonable time.

510. Although a title insurance policy does cover the risk of loss for many reasons, which of the following risks would NOT be covered?

A. Loss due to the failure of a wife to sign the deed on community property
B. An unpaid county property tax not shown in the policy
C. Lack of capacity of a former seller
D. A zoning ordinance, regulation, or plan

511. The process of expressing anticipated future benefits of ownership in dollars, and discounting them to a present worth at a rate that is attracting purchase capital to similar investments is called

A. projection.
B. yield evaluation.
C. equity manipulation.
D. capitalization.

512. If a tenant is evicted unjustly, the tenant may do any of the following, EXCEPT

A. surrender possession and pay no further rent.
B. Sue for possession of the premises.
C. petition the court to appoint a three-man tribunal to arbitrate the matter.
D. sue for damages for wrongful eviction.

513. A broker goes to list a church that was purchased by an unincorporated group in 1972. To be sure that the proper party signs the listing, he should

A. ask the lending institution that lent the money to build the church.
B. ask two former officers of the church.
C. check the by-laws or the charter to see who has authority.
D. ask to see the minutes of the Board of Director's meeting.

514. Assume that after an offer has been accepted, a liquidated damages agreement in the contract had been initialed by both parties. Subsequently, the buyers become convinced they have paid too much for the property and decide to forfeit their deposit which was being held by the broker in his trust account, rather than to go through with the purchase. In such a case

A. the broker could keep all of the deposit, as his commission would have been more than this amount.
B. the seller may choose not to accept the deposit as liquidated damages and sue the buyers for specific performance.
C. broker is entitled to keep half the deposit returning the other half to the buyer.
D. seller can demand the entire deposit from the broker and have no obligation for payment of any commission.

515. Less-than-freehold estates consist of estates owned by

A. trust deed beneficiaries.
B. holders of easements.
C. lessees.
D. grantee of life estates.

516. The fundamental basis for fair housing throughout the United States stems from

A. National Association of License Law Officials.
B. First amendment to the United States Constitution.
C. Thirteenth amendment to the United States Constitution.
D. Rumford Fair Housing Act.

517. An appurtenant easement is

A. an interest in land incapable of transfer.
B. an interest in land capable of transfer.

C. a possession interest in the land of another person.
D. personal to the holder and incapable of transfer.

518. Which of the following may not be added to the original cost basis of real property to arrive at an adjusted basis for federal income tax purposes?

A. Cost of improvements
B. Mortgage payments
C. Miscellaneous acquisition expenses
D. Real estate brokerage commission

519. A husband and wife purchased a residence in 2003 and paid $670,000. After living in the home for more than a year, they sell the property for $630,000. The amount of deduction that they can take for this loss on their federal income tax return would be

A. $4,000.
B. 60%.
C. 40%.
D. nothing.

520. A prospective buyer who was not a real estate licensee, nor had any "ties" with the seller's broker, wished to purchase a large parcel of land and made an offer on the property at a price of $600 per acre. The seller accepted the offer and escrow was opened. During the escrow period the seller discovered that the buyer had already entered into an agreement to resell the acreage at a price of $2,000 per acre to an unknown buyer. Under these circumstances the original seller's recourse is to

A. rescind the contract.
B. refuse to close the escrow and sue for damages.
C. void the contract based on misrepresentation.
D. do nothing.

521. Governmental land use, planning, and zoning are important examples of

A. eminent domain.
B. police power.
C. deed restrictions.
D. all of the above.

522. The "Secondary Mortgage Market" could be best described as

A. junior loans.
B. mortgages passed between mortgagees.
C. mortgages passed between mortgagors.
D. where loans are originated to borrowers.

523. A widow who is willed the use of the family home for the rest of her natural life, with provision that title shall go to the children upon her death, holds a/an

A. fee simple estate.
B. leasehold.
C. easement.
D. life estate.

524. The purchaser of a lot that is subject to a lien for street improvements under the Street Improvement Act of 1911 may prevent the assessment from going to bond if he pays the assessment in full within how many days after the completion of the work?

A. 30 days
B. 60 days
C. 90 days
D. 120 days

525. The Income Approach would not be used when appraising

A. commercial retail properties.
B. residences in a new subdivision.

C. industrial building on a long term lease.
D. neighborhood shopping center.

526. Many real estate contracts allow for writing the terms on forms. Parts of these contracts are written and parts are printed. In the interpretation of such contracts

A. Printed parts take precedence over the written parts.
B. The written parts and the printed parts are given equal consideration.
C. The written parts take precedence over the printed parts.
D. Any parts copied from the form take precedence over those that are purely original.

527. Mrs. Jackson, a real estate developer, subdivides a parcel of land into 50 lots. She receives a Final Public Report to sell. Her first two transactions are to sell five lots to a contractor and also to option five lots to a speculator. Concerning these transactions

A. only the sales need be reported to the Real Estate Commissioner.
B. the subdivider must notify the Real Estate Commissioner of both the sales and the options.
C. only the options must be reported to the Real Estate Commissioner.
D. neither would have to be reported to the Real Estate Commissioner.

528. If a residential neighborhood consists primarily of owner-occupied homes, the immediate economic results would be a

A. raising of housing prices.
B. low turnover of occupants.
C. high potential rental income area.
D. lowering of housing prices.

529. Which of the following expresses the creation of an estate in real property?

A. A lease
B. A bill of sale
C. A trust deed
D. An easement

530. The opposite of alienation is

A. hypothecation.
B. acquisition.
C. subordination.
D. subrogation.

531. A person who hires real property from the owner and is given the exclusive right to use it is known as a

A. tenant.
B. licensee.
C. lodger.
D. boarder.

532. Of the following situations, which would be exempt from the discrimination in housing provisions of the government?

A. The sale of an owner-occupied single-family home that is unencumbered
B. The leasing of a dwelling unit in an owner-occupied four-plex that is unencumbered
C. The leasing of a room to one person in an owner-occupied single-family home that is unencumbered
D. All of the above.

533. A prepayment clause in a mortgage

A. is never lawful.
B. provides for a certain sum to be paid by the mortgagor if the loan is paid off before the maturity date.

C. provides for a penalty in the event of a foreclosure.
D. provides for a penalty payment if the taxes and assessments are not paid on time.

534. An investor purchased a home for $72,000, with a $20,000 down payment and financed the balance with a $52,000 straight note. The investor then sold the property for double the purchase price. If the investor had made no principal or interest payments on the loan, each dollar invested would now be worth

A. $2.20.
B. $4.00.
C. $4.60.
D. $6.60.

535. Under tenancy in common, when one co-tenant dies

A. survivors own his share automatically.
B. his interest passes to his devisees under his will, or to his heirs.
C. the co-owning survivors automatically become executors of his estate.
D. none of the above.

536. The sale of property that is under a long-term lease to another party

A. has no effect upon the term of the lease as far as the tenant is concerned.
B. terminates the lease and the tenant must negotiate a lease with the new owner.
C. terminates the lease upon 30 days notice from the new owner.
D. Cannot be completed until the tenant is notified of the intention to sell and is given the opportunity to terminate the lease.

537. The use of the market data approach to value requires adjustments to be made to often determine value. These adjustments are made as follows

A. subject property is adjusted to the standards set by the comparables.
B. comparables are adjusted to the characteristics of the subject property.
C. subject property is averaged to a range of price.
D. comparables are adjusted to a market norm.

538. A property is listed with your employing broker for $60,000. The property has a loan encumbering it with a balance of $12,000. You discover that the lender will accept a cash pay-off at a 50% discount, that is, he will accept $6,000 immediate cash as full payment. You have a buyer willing to offer $60,000 cash for the property. You should

A. inform the lender that the property is being sold for all cash and he will receive a full $12,000 loan pay-off in escrow.
B. inform the seller that his loan can be paid off prior to the sale at a 50% discount.
C. offer to purchase the loan from the lender at 50% discount, thereby realizing a substantial profit for your broker.
D. say nothing to either side, lender or buyer and allow matters to take their own course.

539. A couple wanted to buy a house for $470,000. The contract contained a contingency clause based on a 100% loan. The bank would only loan $360,000. The buyers had given a $1,500 deposit. The buyers could

A. go to the seller and renegotiate.
B. take the bank's loan and put up the difference.
C. back out and ask for their money back.
D. do any of the above.

540. The broker failed to sign the deposit receipt in the proper place. Which of the following would be true?

A. Either buyer or seller could withdraw from the sale as it is not a binding contract.
B. It would not affect the validity of the deposit receipt.
C. The broker could lose his license.
D. The contract is automatically void.

541. Which of the following could take place before a judgment was issued?

A. Attachment Lien
B. Issuance of a Subpoena
C. Lis Pendens notice
D. Any or all of the above.

542. Which is not a consideration in determining if an item is a fixture?

A. Method of attachment
B. Adaptability of the item to the property
C. Relationship of parties
D. Cost of the item

543. When the public records have been examined in order to determine the Chain of Title to a parcel of real property, a written summary of that Chain of Title is known as

A. an Abstract of Title.
B. an Extended Coverage Title Insurance Policy.
C. an Affidavit of Title.
D. none of the above.

544. The type of deed generally used to clear a "cloud on the title" is

A. Grant Deed.
B. Quitclaim Deed.
C. Warranty Deed.
D. Reconveyance Deed.

545. The Dominant Tenement has a/an

A. lien.
B. easement.
C. license.
D. "cloud" on its title.

546. Which of the following CANNOT be defined as blanket encumbrances according to subdivision laws?

A. Mechanics Liens
B. Trust Deeds
C. Real property taxes
D. Mortgages

547. Warehousing involves

A. corporate trustees.
B. mortgage portfolios.
C. servicing defaulted loans.
D. subdivision development.

548. Which of the following would be the superior or highest lien?

A. A lien created under the provisions of the Street Improvement Act of 1911
B. A recorded deed
C. Whichever is recorded first
D. A Mechanic's Lien

549. Conduit would be used by a/an

A. electrician.
B. roofer.
C. carpenter.
D. plumber.

550. A licensee was attempting to list homes for sale by cautioning owners that minority groups were moving into the area. He mentioned that as a result, property values would decrease, the quality of the schools would suffer, and crime rates would increase. Under these circumstances

A. there has been no violation of the Realtor's Code of Ethics.
B. the Real Estate Commissioner cannot discipline the licensee because he has no jurisdiction even though the licensee is acting unethically.
C. the Real Estate Commissioner can discipline the licensee.
D. if the facts are true, he cannot be disciplined.

551. A broker receives a check as a deposit on a property. Along with the check are written instructions for the broker to hold the check uncashed until acceptance of the offer. The broker should:

A. place the check into the broker's trust account not later than the end of the next working day.
B. hold the check uncashed and inform the seller before seller's decision on the offer that broker is holding the check uncashed.
C. enter the fact of the receipt of the check into the broker's trust fund records and hold the check in a safe place.
D. B and C are correct.

552. An appraiser, while inspecting a house, finds cracks in the wall in a corner of the basement. What is the most likely cause?

A. House has termite infestation.
B. House has settled.
C. House is at least 16 years old.
D. Joists were not strong enough.

553. A policy of TITLE insurance requires a careful search of the public records. The public records covered are found in the

A. county recorder's office.
B. federal land office records.
C. county clerk's office.
D. all of the above.

554. Broker Jones takes a listing on a home. In the listing, the owner states that ABC Escrow is to be used. Broker Jones brings an offer for the property that calls for the escrow to be handled by Golden Coast Escrow. The seller accepts the offer submitted by the broker. Which of the following statements is true?

A. Since the buyer and the seller have requested different escrow companies, the broker should select the escrow company.
B. The buyer must always be given preference in the choice of the escrow company.
C. The seller's choice of escrow companies will be used because the listing was signed first.
D. The escrow should be held by Golden Coast Escrow since the buyer and seller both signed the deposit receipt.

555. Ms. Miller executed a full price and terms offer to purchase Taylor's property through Broker Micks, who held an exclusive authorization and right to sell listing. As the broker was leaving the office to present the offer, another broker handed him a second offer for $1,000 less than the listed sales price but which contained a larger down payment and other different terms. Micks, the listing broker, should

A. tell the other broker that the property has already been sold.

B. present both offers at the same time.
C. present the offers to the seller in the same order that he received them.
D. present the second offer only if the first offeree appears to be a credit risk.

556. If an escrow officer receives two structural pest control reports, the escrow officer should

A. use the most recent report.
B. use the report which discovered the most damage.
C. ask the broker which report he wants to use.
D. submit both reports to the buyer and seller and let them decide which report to use.

557. Which of the following is regarded as a personal property interest?

A. All buildings erected on a parcel
B. A stand of virgin timber
C. Leasehold estates in real property
D. Rights to the unextracted minerals

558. Which of the following real estate loan costs need NOT be disclosed to consumers under the Federal Truth-in-Lending Law?

A. Credit investigations
B. Discount points paid by a buyer
C. Finder's fees
D. The time-price differential

559. How many acres are in the east 1/2 of the north 1/2 of the south 1/2 of the north 1/2 of section 14?

A. 160 acres
B. 80 acres
C. 40 acres
D. 20 acres

560. Which of the following approaches to value tends to set the upper limit of value?

A. Market comparison
B. Replacement cost
C. Income approach
D. Comparable sales method

561. A broker obtained an exclusive right to sell listing on a property. He expended much time, money, and energy trying to sell it. The seller decided he didn't want to sell and refused to allow the broker to proceed under the agreement. Under these circumstances, the broker should

A. ignore the seller and proceed.
B. consider seller's refusal a breach and attempt to relist under new terms.
C. consider the seller's refusal evidence of impossibility to perform, thus relieving seller of liability.
D. consider the seller's refusal a breach and sue for damages.

562. Loan points are charged to

A. allow for competition in the interest rates.
B. adjust fixed rates to make them competitive with non-fixed rates.
C. equalize interest rates.
D. all of the above.

563. Under the provisions of Division 6 of the Uniform Commercial Code, who is protected by the publishing and recording requirements?

A. Creditors
B. Vendors
C. Vendees
D. All of the above.

564. A Quitclaim Deed conveys

A. any interest the grantor may have.
B. a guaranteed title.
C. easements only.
D. trade fixtures.

565. Which of the following acts may legally be taken by a minor or incompetent person in the absence of court approval?

A. Acquire real property through gift or inheritance.
B. Sell the real property through a guardian.
C. Give a valid power of attorney to encumber real property.
D. All of the above.

566. A cautious buyer paid $200 for a four-month option to purchase a property for $30,000. Under these circumstances each of the following is true, EXCEPT the

A. optionee has given legally adequate consideration.
B. optionee has created a legal interest in the property.
C. optionor's temporary surrender of right to sell is "valuable" consideration.
D. agreement imposes no obligation on the optionee to purchase the property.

567. The minimum time required for an owner to give notice to the tenants in an apartment building when that building is being converted by the owner to a condominium form of ownership is

A. 60 days.
B. 120 days.
C. 180 days.
D. 360 days.

568. You are a California real estate broker. A prospect is referred to you by an out-of-state broker and a sale is consummated by you. You want to split your commission with the cooperating broker. Under the California Real Estate Law

A. you may pay a commission to a broker of another state.
B. you cannot divide a commission with a broker of another state.
C. you can pay a commission to a broker of another state only if he or she is also licensed in California.
D. none of the above are correct.

569. The main purpose of indemnifying oneself with a fire insurance policy would be to

A. lose only a small amount.
B. not lose, but possibly gain.
C. always gain.
D. neither lose nor gain.

570. If you have an estate in severalty you have a title as

A. community property.
B. a syndicate.
C. a sole owner.
D. in any form that involves others as co-title owners.

571. The Real Estate Commissioner, when regulating the sale of subdivision land under his control, would be most interested in

A. streets.
B. sewers.
C. financing of the interests in the common grounds.
D. all of the above.

572. Which of the following is most vital or important in planning a subdivision?

A. Market analysis
B. Cost analysis
C. Community recreational analysis
D. Site analysis

573. A prospective buyer would be entitled to damages from a real estate broker in the event the broker

A. makes a representation based on information received from the employing seller.
B. acts in excess of the authority given the broker by the seller.
C. executes a contract in the name of the seller after being properly authorized by a power of attorney.
D. turns the buyer's deposit over to the seller, and thereafter the contract fails without the agent's fault.

574. An apartment building is valued at $300,000 using a 6% capitalization rate. How much would an investor pay for the property if he demanded an 8% capitalization rate?

A. $250,000
B. $225,000
C. $400,000
D. $300,000

575. Lis Pendens is in effect

A. during court proceedings.
B. until disposition of the case.
C. until a judgment of the court has become final.
D. all of the above.

576. Title to personal property is conveyed by a

A. Bill of Sale.
B. Land Contract of Sale.
C. Chattel Mortgage.
D. Deed.

577. An executrix of an estate is

A. appointed by the probate court.
B. named in the decedent's will.
C. selected by the devisee.
D. appointed by the decedent's attorney.

578. Certain activities performed for compensation require a person to hold a real estate license. The following would require a real estate license, provided compensation was sought or received:

A. The negotiation of the sale of real property by a person holding a duly executed Power of Attorney
B. A trustee named in a Trust Deed, selling real property 120 days after a Notice of Default was recorded
C. A corporation officer with a fixed salary who sells the corporation's own real property without receiving any extra compensation
D. Assisting in the filing of an application for the purchase or lease of lands owned by the State or Federal Government

579. An extension of credit by a seller who takes a note and a trust deed is called a

A. Blanket Trust Deed.
B. Hard Money Loan.
C. Land Contract.
D. Purchase Money Trust Deed.

580. Which of the following would be classified as a turnkey project?

A. A vacant lot with complete architectural plans
B. A residential subdivision that is completed and ready for occupancy
C. A low income housing project subsidized by the government
D. An illegal subdivision

581. Which of the following is an advantage of the market data approach to value in the appraising process?

A. It provides an accurate forecast of long-range values.
B. Often comparison properties are numerous.
C. Amenities are easy to compare.
D. It is the simplest of the approaches to learn and to use.

582. When a purchaser under a land contract is paying the seller impounds for taxes and insurance, those payments may not be disbursed for any other purpose without the consent of the

A. trustee.
B. holder in due course.
C. seller.
D. payor.

583. All of the following are common ways to measure the area of a parcel of land EXCEPT

A. square foot.
B. front foot.
C. metes and bounds.
D. acre.

584. A man made an offer to purchase a property together with a deposit, and the broker filled out a deposit receipt form. A copy of the deposit receipt is to be given to the offeror

A. when seller has signed an acceptance to the offer.
B. when broker has returned to his office and typed up additional copies.
C. at the time it is signed by the buyer.
D. together with a copy of the escrow instructions.

585. A salesperson sold a home listed with a broker who is cooperating with her employing broker. She may receive an advance against her commission from the

A. listing broker.
B. listing broker, if she signs a note.
C. listing broker, when the purchase price is deposited in escrow.
D. employing broker.

586. "Placement of the improvement on the lot" is known as

A. orientation.
B. plot plan.
C. plottage.
D. elevation sheet.

587. A man who owned a single family residence was going to put the house on the market. If he wanted to be sure that the buyer would first get the highest possible FHA loan, he could

A. apply to FHA for an appraisal.
B. apply to the lender for a firm commitment.
C. apply for a conditional commitment.
D. send an appraisal to FHA.

588. California law permits a person to file a Declaration of Homestead provided that person is living in

A. a residence on which he or she holds a 35-year lease.
B. a cooperative apartment project in which he or she has a fee interest in the unit.
C. a twelve-unit apartment building which he or she owns.
D. any of the above.

589. You have a prospective buyer for a single family dwelling and the subject of Title Insurance has come up. The buyer states that he wants the greatest protection available to him as an owner. He should request the following

A. a Certificate of Title.
B. Standard Coverage of Title Insurance.
C. an ALTA Policy.
D. Extended Coverage Policy of Title Insurance.

590. A homestead recorded under California law may be invalidated by

A. moving to another state.
B. moving from the property.
C. destruction of the home by fire.
D. a prior homestead on another property.

591. The measure of goods and services produced by the nation during any one calendar year'' is the definition of which of the following?

A. National Economic Conditions
B. Gross National Product
C. Cost of Living Index
D. Business Cycle

592. A licensed real estate broker had a listing on a residence at a price of $120,000. There was no stipulation in the listing contract with regard to deposits of the buyer. The broker advertised the property and received an inquiry from a prospect. After showing the property, the prospective buyer said that he and his wife wanted to make an offer on the property for the full listed price and terms but were not willing to give the broker a deposit with their offer. Under these circumstances the broker should

A. accept offer but should tell the prospective buyer that the offer is possibly void without a deposit.
B. refuse to accept the offer as it is not a legally binding offer without a deposit.
C. refuse the offer as it is a violation of the licensing laws.
D. accept the offer, and present it to the seller but advise the seller there is no deposit.

593. When selling a business opportunity, the seller must collect sales tax from the buyer on which of the following items?

A. The inventory which is included in the sale
B. The fixtures and furniture included with the business
C. "Goodwill" value
D. None of the above

594. Which of the following would be classified as economic obsolescence?

A. An oversupply of like properties
B. Lack of on-site parking
C. Poorly designed rooms
D. Deteriorated roofing

595. Which of the following is not a soil condition or type of soil?

A. Expansive
B. Adobe
C. Alkaline
D. Deciduous

596. Every licensee who sells a real property sales contract shall cause a proper assignment of the contract to be executed and shall cause the assignment to be recorded in the county in which the real property is located within the following number of days after close of escrow?

A. Within 30 days
B. Within 10 days
C. Never
D. None of the above.

597. Which of the following is required to obtain a California Real Estate Salesperson's License?

A. U.S. citizenship
B. Be 18 years of age
C. Be a resident of California
D. Obtain score of 100% on license exam

598. On a construction loan, the last payment by the lender is usually made

A. when the building is completed.
B. upon proof of recording of the notice of completion.
C. before the house is sold.
D. after the lien period has expired.

599. A Grant Deed in California always contains

A. two express warranties.
B. two implied warranties.
C. grantee's signature.
D. street address of the property.

600. A person delegated in an instrument to act legally for another, in his stead, is known as which of the following?

A. Fiduciary
B. Principal
C. Attorney in fact
D. Power of Attorney

601. A family of three siblings, all grown, can take title as

A. tenants in common.
B. joint tenants.
C. a partnership.
D. Any of the above.

602. Barry took a listing without ever inspecting the property. A buyer saw the sign, the owner showed the buyer the property, whereupon the buyer immediately entered into an escrow with the seller. Escrow closed. Which of the following statements is correct?

A. Barry has not violated any law.
B. Since there were no problems with the property, no one was hurt, no harm no foul.
C. No one will ever know.
D. Barry should have inspected the home as required by law. Barry could lose his real estate brokers license for this act of negligence.

603. An easement:

A. Is a possessory interest in the dominant tenement.
B. Can be terminated with a merger of the dominant and servient tenement.
C. Can be treated only by a deed.
D. Can be distinguished from a license because a license is a non-possessory interest.

604. Which of the following would receive the most emphasis in an appraisal to place a value on a three-year old home for fire insurance purposes?

A. The cost approach
B. The income approach
C. The market approach
D. An average of all of the above.

605. Copies of all listings, deposit receipts, and trust records must be retained by a licensed real estate broker for

A. one year.
B. two years.
C. three years.
D. four years.

606. A landlord of a commercial building and a tenant enter into a lease agreement with the rent specified at $300 per month for the entire term of the lease. This type of lease is often very lengthy with many different clauses, especially if it is a commercial lease. Which of the following clauses would be LEAST likely to be found in such a contract?

A. Security for performance
B. Compliance with government laws
C. Condemnation
D. Escalator

607. In the absence of any agreement respecting the length of time of the rent, the hiring is presumed to be

A. daily.
B. weekly.
C. monthly (month to month).
D. annually.

608. Normally a deed deposited in escrow may be delivered to the grantee

A. immediately.
B. upon payment of equity to the seller.
C. only upon the performance of all conditions of the escrow.
D. upon the request of the real estate broker.

609. An estate of indefinite duration is a/an

A. An estate of inheritance.
B. An estate for years.
C. A lease for 99 years.
D. A month to month tenancy.

610. Every lease contains an implied covenant of "quiet enjoyment and possession." This covenant directly relates to:

A. A title that is free of all encumbrances.
B. Tenant's possession free of disturbances by the landlord or another who has paramount title.
C. Nuisances inflicted by adjoining neighbors.
D. Liability for damages due to tenant's negligence.

611. An earned commission may be kept in a broker's trust fund for no more than

A. one day.
B. seven days.
C. thirty days.
D. sixty days.

612. A wife's separate property, without a will, would be distributed as follows,

A. all to the children.
B. half to the children and half the surviving spouse.

C. all to the surviving spouse.
D. one third to the surviving spouse and two thirds to the children if more than one child.

613. During 1968, Congress adopted Open Housing legislation to guard against discrimination in the sale and rental of housing in this country, because of race, creed, color, religion, or national original. The federal authority charged with the responsibility of administering this legislation is the

A. Department of Health, Education and Welfare.
B. U.S. Attorney General's Office.
C. Department of Housing and Urban Development.
D. Department of Consumer Affairs.

614. The owner-operator of a large retail store sold the building that housed his business and immediately leased back the property from the new owner on a long-term basis. Several advantages are realized by the business operator in such a lease-back arrangement. Most important of which is

A. relief from the problems of property management.
B. increased working capital.
C. rental payments are deductible as a business expense.
D. the hazard of increased property taxes is lessened.

615. To alienate title to property, one

A. encumbers the title.
B. clouds the title.
C. records a homestead.
D. conveys title.

616. A real estate licensee was actively seeking listings by contacting owners in a non-integrated neighborhood and telling them that minorities were moving into the area and as a result, the values of homes in the area would suffer a loss in value and it was a good time to sell their property. This type of activity by the licensee would be considered

A. steering.
B. inducement of panic selling.
C. blockbusting.
D. both B and C.

617. Which of the following would be used to transfer a title or interest in trade fixtures when selling a business?

A. A negotiable instrument
B. A Chattel Real
C. A Bill of Sale
D. None of the above

618. One of the distinguishing economic characteristics of real property is that it is

A. Immovable.
B. A long-term investment.
C. Very costly.
D. Likely to increase in value.

619. Under the real estate law, certain requirements have been imposed on brokers engaged in the business of negotiating mortgage loans, including the requirements of securing a borrower's signature to a mortgage loan broker statement. The period of time during which he must keep this statement on file for inspection is

A. 90 days after transaction is completed and funds distributed to borrower.

B. three years from date the instrument was signed by the borrower.
C. one year from date the loan was secured.
D. one years from date originally fixed for the termination of the note secured by the trust deed.

620. Mr. Jackson owned two acres of land. He sold one acre to Mr. Johnson but retained an easement across Mr. Johnson's acre for a road. Jackson used the road for a while and later abandoned it. Five years later he wants to reopen the roadway, but Johnson refuses to permit him to do so

A. Johnson has the right to do this.
B. the easement is now invalid since it was not used for five years.
C. the easement is valid and has not been outlawed.
D. the easement will expire in ten years.

621. The Health and Safety Code of the State of California contains a statement that opposes the practice of discrimination due to race, color, religion, national origin, or ancestry in publicly assisted housing accommodations. Property considered to be included in the term "publicly-assisted housing" would be

A. housing granted tax exemptions, except for the veteran's exemption.
B. housing built on land sold at low cost by a state or local agency pursuant to the Federal Housing Act of 1949.
C. housing located in a multiple dwelling on which there is a loan insured by a government agency.
D. any of the above.

622. The State sales tax due on the fixtures in the sale of a business opportunity is

A. paid by the buyer to the seller together with the purchase price.
B. remitted by the seller to the State Board of Equalization.
C. paid before the Certificate of Clearance is issued.
D. all of the above.

623. A homestead exemption recorded after court action has been instituted but not concluded is

A. valid.
B. void.
C. unenforceable.
D. ineffective as to after recorded judgments.

624. When a salesperson terminates employment with a broker, the license should be

A. given to the salesperson and notice be given to the Commissioner of the termination.
B. torn up by the broker.
C. given to the salesperson and nothing further be done by the broker.
D. sent to the commissioner by the broker.

625. A seller who has owned his property for three years offers the property to a buyer that is buying with all cash. The seller is most likely to pay a prepayment penalty if he has which of the following types of loans?

A. VA
B. FHA
C. Hard money second trust deed
D. Conventional

626. Which of the following words are synonymous?

A. Take-out loan - interim loan
B. Construction loan - interim loan
C. Take-out loan - construction loan
D. Short term loan - take-out loan

627. Mr. Jones told broker Bob, "While I will not sign a listing on my home, if you can find a buyer who will pay at least $250,000 for it, I'll pay you 6% commission." Three weeks later, broker Bob found a buyer who gave him a $1,000 deposit on the purchase price of $265,000, along with a signed offer to purchase. When the offer was presented to Mr. Jones, he accepted it and then demanded that the deposit be given to him. Which of the following is true?

A. Once the offer is accepted, the deposit belongs to the seller without the buyer's written consent.
B. Broker Bob may not give the buyer's deposit to the seller without the buyer's written consent.
C. Because the listing was not in writing, broker Bob is not obligated to follow the seller's orders.
D. Broker Bob should deposit the money in escrow and then let the escrow officer worry about it.

628. If a listing contract does not authorize the agent to accept deposit money on behalf of the seller, the agent accepts the money as

A. agent for the seller, always.
B. agent for an escrow company.
C. agent for the buyer.
D. as a neutral escrow depository.

629. When property is being purchased and financed by a new loan through the Cal-Vet loan program, the seller will (in order to consummate the sale and have the chain of title read correctly), execute a grant deed to the

A. escrow agent, to be held in trust for the veteran buyer.
B. trustee designated in the deed of trust.
C. Department of Veterans Affairs.
D. veteran purchaser who assigns an equitable title to the Department of Veterans Affairs.

630. In the preparation of an exclusive right to sell listing contract, the following would NOT be interpreted as a date of final and complete termination

A. until two months from the date hereof.
B. for a period of 90 days and thereafter for a further period of three months, during which period either party may terminate on five days' notice.
C. for a period of 60 days and thereafter until five days' notice of termination is given by either party.
D. for a period of 60 days during which either party may give five days' notice of termination.

631. Restrictions in a deed prohibit the use or construction that is allowed in a zoning ordinance. Which prevails?

A. The deed restriction
B. The master planning commission plan
C. The zoning ordinance
D. Whichever was recorded first

632. Mr. Miller lives at the bottom of a hill. During heavy rains, surface water from above almost engulfs his home. Mr. Miller dug a trench along the back of his lot and diverted the water away from his land on to a nearby vacant lot. His action was

A. legal because any person may protect himself from flood water overflowing a defined channel.
B. legal because no damage could occur by diverting water to a vacant lot.
C. illegal because a person may not disturb the flow of surface water and divert it on to another property.
D. illegal because a person may not obstruct surface waters unless a permit is obtained from the flood control district.

633. A veteran wanted to purchase a home for $350,000. The VA appraised the property for $342,000. The veteran could

A. put $8,000 down and get a $342,000 loan.
B. cannot buy, as he can only borrow $342,000.
C. can only buy the property if the appraised value is at least $350,000.
D. could get a second loan for $8,000 and borrow $342,000.

634. The most logical first step in land development is

A. an analysis of the market.
B. the determination of development cost.
C. the acquisition of land.
D. a decision regarding location of project.

635. If the Federal Reserve Bank feels that there is an inflationary trend developing in the United States they can do which of the following?

A. Adjust the amount of reserves required for its member banks
B. Increase the discount rate
C. Enter into the government bond market in a selling capacity
D. All of the above

636. Which of the four major characteristics that create value would be the LEAST important?

A. Demand
B. Transferability
C. Scarcity
D. Utility

637. A Declaration of Homestead may not be filed on a property that

A. is already encumbered by a trust deed or mortgage.
B. has a value in excess of $30,000.
C. is not community property.
D. is not occupied by the declarant (or person declaring the homestead) at the time of filing.

638. Which of the following would be considered a valid delivery of a deed?

A. The escrow officer mailed the deed, which was acknowledged by the seller, and the delivery had been made after the seller had died.
B. The escrow company had delivered the deed to the buyers prior to the buyer meeting all the terms of the escrow.
C. The grantee was delivered the deed after the grantor's death in accordance with the grantor's instructions left with his attorney.
D. The seller had handed the deed to the buyer but the buyer failed to record the deed.

639. In order for a deed to be valid and convey title, the following is required

A. execution on a day of the week other than Sunday.
B. a property description.
C. use of the phrase "to have and to hold."
D. an acknowledgment.

640. The Real Estate Commissioner would most likely deny a Public Report if the subdivision plans included

A. individual water systems for each lot.
B. the use of septic tanks.
C. a private road.
D. the development of recreational facilities without adequate and available financing.

641. The interest rate on one of the following types of financing might be changed during the term of the loan

A. FHA.
B. Cal-Vet.
C. G.I.
D. none of the above.

642. If a borrower defaults on an FHA insured loan, any losses sustained in foreclosures are made up through

A. an attachment lien against the borrower.
B. an assessment against the lending institution.
C. a mutual mortgage insurance plan.
D. the Federal Treasury.

643. Members of city and county planning commissions are

A. elected in cities and appointed in counties.
B. appointed in cities and elected in counties.
C. required by law to have experience in real estate and subdivisions.
D. authorized to make recommendations to City Council or Board of Supervisors regarding subdivisions.

644. Which of the following agencies has jurisdiction over the Interstate Land Sales Full Disclosure Act?

A. Federal Trade Commission
B. Department of Housing and Urban Development
C. U.S. Department of Interior
D. State licensing authority

645. A broker who discharges a salesperson for misconduct in connection with the handling of a real estate transaction must file a certified statement of the facts in the matter with the Real Estate Commissioner

A. within 10 days of such discharge.
B. immediately.
C. within 30 days.
D. none of the above.

646. Which of the following describes the conscious charging by a private lender of more than the maximum amount of interest allowed by law?

A. Usury
B. Penury
C. Assemblage
D. Leverage

647. The relationship between the thing desired and the potential purchaser is best defined as

A. the present worth as opposed to future income.
B. value.
C. the relationship between utility and value.
D. the relationship between demand and value.

648. Which of the following types of depreciation is usually the most difficult to cure?

A. Functional obsolescence
B. Physical obsolescence
C. Economic obsolescence
D. Physical deterioration

649. Mr. Smith, a veteran, makes an offer to purchase a property for $75,000, and gives the broker $500 cash as a deposit and to cover the closing costs of the purchase. The offer was made contingent upon his ability to obtain a VA loan for the amount of the purchase price. If the seller accepts the offer and a CRV is obtained on the property for $73,000, the buyer may

A. offer the seller an additional $2,000 cash down payment and complete the sale.
B. re-negotiate the purchase of the property with the seller for a lower price.
C. recover his $500 cash deposit.
D. any of the above.

650. Jones wanted a friend, Bill Harris, to have his property if he failed to return from a planned trip. He acknowledged a Grant Deed, naming Bill Harris as grantee, and left it in his desk. Jones' son-in-law, also named Bill Harris, found the deed and had it recorded. The legal owner would be

A. son-in-law Harris.
B. friend Harris.
C. both A and B.
D. neither A nor B.

651. In California, the use of an Abstract of Title has been superseded almost entirely by the

A. title guarantee.
B. certificate of title.
C. trust deed.
D. policy of title insurance.

652. When calculating the budget for a real estate office, the term "Company Dollar" refers to

A. the income of an office after all expenses have been subtracted.
B. the income of an office after all commissions have been subtracted.
C. the money required to open an office and run it for a specific period of time.
D. none of the above.

653. Owner Armstrong gave Broker Weeks an exclusive authorization to sell Armstrong's ranch. As part of the agreement, Broker Weeks agreed to advertise the ranch in a catalog that Weeks publishes and distributes to other real estate brokers. For this added service, Armstrong paid Broker Weeks $1,000 at the time Owner Armstrong signed the listing. Under current real estate law, this payment

A. must be deposited into a trust account under an agreement that may provide for forfeiture by Owner Armstrong if the owner breaches the listing agreement.
B. may be cashed or deposited by Broker Weeks, but records must reflect disposition of such funds.
C. must be retained by Broker Weeks in a trust fund account so that it may be refunded to Owner Armstrong if the property is not sold by the broker during the listing term.
D. must be deposited into a trust account and disbursed only to pay advertising expenditures incurred by Broker Weeks in advertising the ranch property.

654. Allen, who owns Greenacres Ranch, leases the property to Taylor for a 10-year term. Allen has signed a will that stated that all his interest in Greenacres Ranch would go to his friend Barnhill. Shortly after executing the lease, Allen died. During the probate proceedings, the will was held to be invalid and void. It was also discovered that Allen had no living heirs. Under these circumstances, Greenacres Ranch

A. passes to Barnhill.
B. passes to the county after five years.
C. passes to Taylor.
D. escheats to the state subject to the lease.

655. When making the building inspection, the appraiser

A. always looks for the same things other appraisers do.
B. considers the purpose of the appraisal.
C. keeps in mind the value approaches to be used.
D. both B and C.

656. With which type of loan is a Certificate of Reasonable Value?

A. Cal-Vet
B. VA
C. FHA
D. Conventional

657. The most likely term used to describe a prospective buyer when dealing with the listing broker is

A. a client.
B. a customer.
C. a trustee.
D. none of the above.

658. The seller must provide the buyer with a real estate transfer disclosure statement in which of the following transactions?

A. A sale of a four unit residential building
B. A bankruptcy sale
C. A trustee sale
D. A transfer between husband and wife

659. Assume that two months after the close of escrow for the sale of property at $80,000, the seller learns for the first time that the buyers were mother and stepfather of the broker, and that an escrow for resale of the property at $95,000 had been signed before their escrow was closed. The seller files a complaint with the Real Estate Commissioner. In your opinion

A. after a hearing, the Commissioner would discipline the broker for not disclosing the relationship and would award money damages to the seller.
B. since the seller got his asking price, there is not basis for a complaint.

C. the Real Estate Law does not cover a situation of this kind and the Commissioner has no jurisdiction.
D. the seller would sue the broker in Civil Court for the amount of profit realized on the resale of the property, and the broker is subject to disciplinary action by the Commissioner.

660. Mrs. Fields held a life estate in a single-family residence. The estate was based upon her own life. She leased the residence to Mr. Fine for a five-year period, but died a few weeks after the lease began. The lease was

A. invalid on its face, because the holder of a life estate does not have the right to lease the property.
B. valid for the remaining term of the lease.
C. valid only during the life of the designated life.
D. valid only if Mr. Fine was unaware of the life estate when the lease was created.

661. The most favorable type of lease to be entered into by the owner of an improved business property in an area that is rapidly gaining in population is a

A. percentage lease based on gross business done, with a minimum guaranteed rental, the lessee to pay the taxes.
B. percentage lease based on the net earnings of the business, with a minimum rental, the lessee to pay the taxes.
C. straight long-term lease at a fixed rental which provides for the tenant to pay the taxes.
D. year to year lease, the rent to be determined by annual pedestrian traffic counts.

662. Which of the following would not be classified as obsolescence?

A. Outdated fixtures
B. Declining neighborhood
C. Wear and tear
D. Misplaced improvements

663. An owner is selling a property at 238 Main Street. She would like to purchase another property and draw up an offer conditional upon the sale of her property. The clause most satisfactory to her would be

A. on condition the escrow closes.
B. on condition the sales escrow is completed.
C. purchase is contingent upon the sale escrow on 238 Main Street closing within 20 days of the date of this offer.
D. on condition the sales escrow concerning the property at 238 Main Street is closed.

664. If the Government obtained a lien against a taxpayer who failed to report a certain portion of his rental income, it would be classified as

A. general.
B. voluntary.
C. specific.
D. none of the above.

665. Which of the following is correct with regard to an enforceable standard listing agreement that has been signed by the seller and the broker?

A. It obligates the seller to sell.
B. It requires a meeting of the minds.
C. It requires a seller able to deliver a marketable title and a buyer be "ready, willing and able" to buy.
D. All of the above.

666. The number of square feet in a home is computed by means of

A. outside measurements of house and garage.
B. inside measurements of house as a whole.
C. inside measurements of each room.
D. outside measurements of house as a whole.

667. An instrument which usually transfers possession of real property, but does not transfer ownership is a/an

A. mortgage.
B. sublease.
C. security agreement.
D. easement.

668. Under a lease for three years, if the tenant remains in possession and the owner accepts payment of rent after the expiration of the term without other agreement or notice to vacate, the lease

A. is cancelled.
B. is renewed for three years.
C. is renewed for one year.
D. becomes a month-to-month tenancy.

669. An appraiser in analyzing the data for his final estimate of value on a property would give least consideration to

A. the assessed value of the property.
B. the value of the land.
C. comparisons of the properties.
D. its highest and best use.

670. Tyson owns a store building that he leased to Crown for seven years. Crown's estate in the store building is

A. personal property.
B. estate for years.
C. a Chattel Real.
D. all of the above.

671. How long does a victim have to file a complaint about discrimination with the Department of Fair Employment and Housing?

A. 30 days
B. 45 days
C. 60 days
D. 90 days

672. Under the Civil Rights Act of 1968, Title VIII, persons complaining of discrimination in housing have the choice of which of the following remedies?

A. File a civil action in Federal Court.
B. File a civil action in state or local court.
C. File a complaint with HUD.
D. Any of the above.

673. A roof with four sloping sides rising to the ridge board is what type

A. flat.
B. hip.
C. gable.
D. gambrel.

674. Naked legal title is held by the

A. mortgagor.
B. beneficiary.
C. trustor.
D. trustee.

675. Which of the following expenses would NEVER be found on the Uniform Settlement Statement form issued at the closing of a RESPA covered transaction?

A. Appraisal fee
B. Finder's fee paid by a lender to a real estate broker.
C. Discount points
D. Title Report

676. Apple grants an estate to Banana for the life of Coconut. If Banana dies while Coconut is still alive, the estate

A. goes to Coconut for his life.
B. reverts to Apple.
C. ceases to exist.
D. goes to the heirs of Banana.

677. A seller listed his property with a broker for $40,000. The listing said, "Seller agrees to pay the broker a 6% commission upon sale. If the buyer defaults, I will pay 1/2 of any damages I may collect, or 6% of the selling price, whichever is less." The broker found a buyer at the listed price who made an offer with a deposit of 1% that was accepted. The buyer later defaulted and forfeited his deposit. The broker would receive

A. $200.
B. $600.
C. $2,400.
D. none of the above.

678. In the sale of a property encumbered with a Deed of Trust, who would have the most liability?

A. Grantor selling subject to the loan
B. Grantee buying subject to the loan
C. Grantee who takes title subject to a loan the grantor has assumed
D. Grantee who assumes a loan from grantor who had taken title subject to the loan

679. A tenant is justified in abandoning a leased property if the landlord demonstrates constructive eviction. Which of the following facts would be considered constructive eviction?

A. The property has been shown to another party and has entered into negotiations with the landlord.
B. The landlord has failed to make needed repairs and maintain the property in the agreed manner.
C. The landlord has altered the building to an extent that it is no longer usable for its original purpose.
D. All of the above.

680. A person holding title to real property in severalty would have

A. a life estate.
B. an estate for years.
C. ownership in common with others.
D. sole ownership.

681. Which of the following statements concerning acknowledgment is TRUE?

A. A notary may acknowledge a deed to property he is purchasing.
B. Deeds drawn and acknowledged out of state are valid.
C. Acknowledgment is a requirement for the validity of a deed.
D. Valid acknowledgment constitutes delivery of a deed.

682. After a "Notice of Default" has been recorded in a foreclosure, the trustee must wait three months before

A. reinstating the loan.
B. taking possession of the property.
C. deeding the title to the beneficiary.
D. advertising a "Notice of Sale."

683. One of the benefits to the seller under a sale-leaseback transaction would be that

A. Any capital gain is tax deferred.
B. Future rent will be fully deductible for incomes taxes purposes.

C. A new tax base is established.
D. The property becomes maintenance expense free.

684. Which of the following can be appurtenant to the land?

A. An attachment
B. Trade fixtures
C. Stock in a mutual water company
D. None of the above

685. The section number that is due west of section 18 is section number

A. 13.
B. 17.
C. 19.
D. 24.

686. If a court proceeding is entered into over a commission split between two licensed real estate brokers, the brokers need not show the court a written contract between them regarding the commission split because

A. it is judicial recognition that this is a common practice between cooperating brokers.
B. no listing agreement or commission agreement need be in writing to be enforceable in court.
C. this type of agreement is not covered under the Statute of Frauds.
D. the Real Estate Law exempts these contracts.

687. A new well and pump were installed on a vacant parcel of land. For assessment purposes, the tax assessor would consider these as

A. improvements.
B. additions.
C. part of the land value.
D. personal property.

688. A seller wanting to relieve himself of the primary liability for payment of a Trust Deed and note must find a buyer who is willing to

A. assume the Trust Deed and note liability.
B. execute a Subordination Agreement.
C. sign a Release Agreement.
D. take title subject to the Trust Deed and note.

689. If a person buys property in a California land project and then changes his mind, he can obtain a refund of his money without a specific reason within how long?

A. 3 calendar days
B. 5 calendar days
C. 10 calendar days
D. 14 calendar days

690. The main purpose of the Real Estate Settlement Procedures Act is to

A. place a fixed limit on settlement costs in all real estate transactions.
B. place a fixed limit on settlement costs on residential property of four units or less.
C. to standardize settlement services throughout the United States.
D. to provide consumers with enough information to enable them to shop for settlement services.

691. In the event of a sale of a retail business, it is necessary to pay state sales tax on

A. furniture and fixtures sold.
B. goodwill.
C. stock transferred.
D. none of the above.

692. A licensed real estate salesperson is handling a transaction where there is an assignment of real property sales contract. He must see that this is recorded within

A. no specified time limit.
B. 30 working days.
C. 10 working days.
D. 5 working days.

693. In the sale of residential real estate the terms and conditions of the sale would usually affect the property's

A. insured value.
B. cost.
C. depreciation.
D. price.

694. In the appraising process, the term "highest and best use" often comes into play. This can best be defined as

A. developing a lot so as to contribute to the best interest of the community.
B. producing the greatest net return on the investment over a period of time.
C. developing a lot so as to produce the highest gross income.
D. all of the above.

695. Where there are local minimum building code requirements, builders must

A. comply only with local and state housing codes.
B. comply only with federal housing specifications.
C. comply with the more stringent of the local, state, or federal laws.
D. observe neither state or federal laws.

696. An owner of real property allows you the right to enter onto their property, but only as long as they wish to do so. This is known as

A. an easement.
B. a right of way.
C. a license.
D. none of the above.

697. Every lease contains an implied covenant of "quiet enjoyment and possession." This covenant directly relates to

A. a title that is free of all encumbrances.
B. tenant's possession free of disturbance by the landlord or another who has paramount title.
C. nuisances inflicted by adjoining neighbors.
D. liability for damages due to tenant's negligence.

698. Whenever a broker is authorized to negotiate for the sale of property

A. he is always authorized to accept a deposit as agent of the seller.
B. unless he is authorized by the seller to accept a deposit, he must refuse to be responsible for accepting a deposit from a buyer.
C. if he accepts a deposit from a buyer without being authorized to do so by the seller, he violates the Real Estate Law.
D. if he accepts a deposit from a buyer without being authorized to do so by the seller, he becomes the agent of the buyer for the purpose of holding the deposit.

699. Under a Land Contract or Agreement of Sale

A. title is transferred to the buyer at the time the contract is signed.
B. if buyer defaults in the payments he has three months plus 21 days in which to reinstate from the date of Notice of Default.
C. seller retains title and may use it as security for a mortgage or trust deed loan to the extent of his equity.
D. buyer may be liable for a deficiency judgment in the event of foreclosure by court action.

700. Broker Smith secured a listing on an older-type dwelling converted to income units. Smith found a prospective purchaser, Mrs. Doe, who expressed great interest in the property. Mrs. Doe is concerned as to whether or not officials might approach her, after purchase, with demands for certain alterations or structural requirements, causing large monetary outlay. The agency that should be contacted to secure reassurance on this point is

A. Local Planning Commission.
B. Local Health Officer.
C. State Contractors License Board.
D. Local Building Department.

701. The broker who most likely has earned a commission is the one who has

A. communicated acceptance to offeror.
B. communicated offer to seller.
C. secured acceptance to an offer.
D. secured a substantial deposit with an offer.

702. Which of the following is the least desirable feature to an investor who is interested in leverage?

A. Continuity of a satisfactory income stream
B. A low interest, fully amortized mortgage
C. Stable business conditions
D. Low interest, short term financing

703. Which of the following are ways by which a landlord can evict a delinquent tenant?

A. Calling the sheriff
B. Giving him thirty days notice
C. Giving a three days notice
D. Bring court action

704. As regards the Real Estate Settlements Procedures Act (RESPA)

A. the buyer must be given the costs upon application for the loan not more than three days from the application or no more than three days thereafter.
B. the borrower/purchaser must be allowed the right by the escrow agent to inspect the finalized Uniform Settlements Statement one day prior to escrow closing, unless they sign a waiver.
C. should the lender or escrow company require the use of a particular title insurance company and receive any referral fees they could be subjected to a fine and possible imprisonment.
D. all of the above are correct statements.

705. The income from real property that is discovered by an examination of properties in an area where the appraiser has determined highest and best use would be

A. developed rent.
B. contract rent plus differential.
C. economic rent.
D. maximized rent.

706. An increase in unemployment within a city has caused an overall reduction of income of the residents. As a result of these conditions, homes in the area are decreasing in value. This decrease in value is referred to as

A. physical deterioration.
B. functional Obsolescence.
C. economic Obsolescence.
D. none of the above.

707. Quite often the Real Estate Commissioner is concerned with compaction when approving a subdivision for sale. This would refer to

A. expansive soil.
B. earth fill.
C. percolation.
D. amount of moisture in lumber used.

708. When a legal description begins with the phrase, "Beginning at a point on the northerly edge of M Street 100 feet easterly of the NE corner of the intersection of M and Seventh Streets, and running thence…," which of the following methods of land description is being used?

A. U.S. Geographical Survey System
B. Recorded Tract Map System
C. U.S. Government Rectangular Survey System
D. Metes and Bounds

709. After Mrs. Gardner purchased her home, she discovered by survey that her neighbor's fence was three feet over her newly acquired property. For remedy, if a friendly settlement cannot be made, she should bring civil suit against

A. the broker, for failure to disclose the encroachment.
B. her neighbor, for removal of the encroachment on the grounds of trespass.
C. her neighbor, under the law of adverse possession.
D. the title company, for failure to show an encumbrance on the standard form title report.

710. An easement

A. is a possessory interest in the dominant tenement.
B. can be terminated with a merger of the dominant and servient tenement.
C. can be created only by a deed.
D. can be distinguished from a license because a license is a non-possessory interest.

711. Upon payment of a fee, certified copies of inspection reports issued by any licensed structural pest control operator may be obtained from the Structural Pest Control Board by

A. seller only.
B. buyer only.
C. seller and Buyers only.
D. anyone.

712. Many items are subject to proration in the real property sale escrow. Buyers and sellers using escrow normally agree to a proration of which of the following?

A. Title insurance fees
B. The cost of corrective termite work

C. The cost of documentary transfer tax
D. Rent

713. The Mortgage Loan Disclosure Statement must contain all of the following EXCEPT

A. a statement of all liens against the property as disclosed by borrower.
B. maximum costs and expenses as estimated by the broker.
C. a credit rating on the borrower.
D. estimated amounts to be paid on order of borrower.

714. A listing contract usually authorizes a broker to

A. convey the real property that is the subject of the listing.
B. find a purchaser and accept a deposit with an offer to purchase.
C. find a purchaser and bind his principal to a contract to sell.
D. assure a prospective purchaser that an offer meeting the terms of the listing will be accepted by his principal.

715. When a veteran purchases property under the Cal-Vet Program, the title to the property is in the name of the

A. Veterans Administration.
B. Veteran.
C. Department of Veterans Affairs.
D. The previous owner until paid in full.

716. A contract for the sale of community real property signed by the wife only is

A. valid.
B. voidable.
C. illegal.
D. void.

1. B. The original three-year contract is no longer in effect, and when the broker accepts additional rent, it creates a periodic tenancy.

2. C. A Prescriptive easement is acquired through adverse use of another's property for a five-year, continuous period. From the facts given in the statement it would appear that this is an easement by prescription.

3. C. Value is subjective depending on an individual's needs. There are four elements to value: demand, utility, scarcity and transferability. Value increases when there is high demand for the same product, creating utility for that product. Value further increases when the product is scarce, creating more demand than supply. Finally value increases when the product is highly transferable from one party to another. The worth, usefulness and utility of a product is subjective, however driven by the four elements of value.

4. A. An option is not an interest in property; it is a unilateral contract in which the optionor is bound, but the optionee is not.

5. D. Original cost has very little or nothing to do in any cost appraisal of an older structure.

6. D. The Uniform Settlement Statement must be delivered to the borrower at, or before, closing. Should the borrower waive this right, and not be present at closing, the statement should be delivered as soon as possible after the transaction closes.

7. D. The Department of Housing and Urban Development enforces fair housing laws on the federal level. Complaints must be filed within one year.

8. B. "Value" can be defined as "present worth of future benefits."

9. A. In popular usage, devise means death. In real estate, it means a transfer real property under a will.

10. D. Basis, cost, cost basis, and purchase price, plus adjustments for capital improvements and deductions for depreciation expense can all be defined as what was paid for the property.

11. B. This is the definition of a condominium. The individual has a fee ownership of the unit and joint ownership of the land and common areas. The key wording is "separate interest in the unit." A community apartment project allows for use or occupation only of the unit.

12. A. A listing is an employment contract hiring the broker to do a job.

13. B. A mortgage is merely an interest in property. An estate refers to an interest in the land whether as an owner or a lessee.

14. A. The important effect of a "sale to the state" by the tax collector is that it starts the redemption period running; however, the delinquent owner's possession remains undisturbed for five years.

15. B. The mortgagor (buyer/borrower) would sign the note and mortgage in favor of the lender. The seller, owner or grantor sells the property, the trustee holds the title in trust, and the mortgagee (lender) takes the mortgage.

16. A. The vast majority of money loaned out through banks and credit unions is the depositors' money placed with their institution. Therefore, the source of the money is individual savings.

17. B. These are the two legal requirements for a valid escrow in California.

18. A. A testament is another word for a will. A male person who makes a will is a testator.

19. A. The original cost of the materials has very little to do with value.

20. A. Population and high traffic count are helpful, but it is important that the residents in the area have good purchasing power.

21. A. When a contract is voidable, one of the parties may reject it because there is a deficiency (defect) in the contract that injures him or her. The injured party may proceed with the contract, but also has the option to disaffirm it (have the court terminate the contract).

22. B. Short blocks are expensive because more land is devoted to streets.

23. D. It is also called "plottage." In appraising it is an important factor influencing value.

24. B. The sole purpose of a trust deed is to secure the note. It is used to place real property as security in the event of nonpayment on the note. The note is the incident of the debt. A trust deed is not held by the trustor (borrower), but rather, it is given by the trustor and held by the beneficiary (lender).

25. A. When an appraiser is concerned with equilibrium and decline of value, she is concerned about the neighborhood; whether it be residential, commercial, industrial or agricultural. The surrounding area is what she would be considering.

26. D. As the loan is paid off, the amount due for interest will decrease, thereby allowing more to be applied to the principal.

27. A. The beneficiary benefits from an impound account by being assured that the taxes and insurance will be paid. The trustor benefits by being relieved of the responsibility to come up with those major costs when taxes and insurance become due.

28. B. Any easement is a burden on servient land. Because an easement in gross belongs to a person, adjacent land would not be involved. There is no dominant tenement.

29. D. A straight note may be secured by a mortgage when it is used in a real estate transaction. It is also a note providing that the entire principal is to be paid at maturity of the loan.

30. A. Recording gives constructive notice to everyone.

31. D. Since the interests are unequal and the fact that the husband acquired title at a later date, it places the brother as tenant in common.

32. C. A Trustee's Sale is an out-of-court foreclosure; a Certificate of Sale is issued to the highest bidder at a mortgage foreclosure; a Writ of Possession is issued to the landlord after a successful judgment in an unlawful detainer action.

33. D. Under the California Subdivision Law, a subdivision of fifty or more lots or parcels is not considered to be a land project if: the lots are not to be offered for sale by means of substantial direct mail advertising, sales promotion costs are nominal; and all lots are to be offered for sale to builders or developers only rather than the general public.

34. A. A deed transfers title to real property; a Bill of Sale transfers title to personal property.

35. B. One yard = 3 feet. Convert 45 feet to 15 yards. 540 square yards / 15 yards = 36 yards. Convert 36 yards to 108 feet.

36. B. The use of a small sum of money to manipulate a large investment, thereby gaining the inflationary increase on the large investment, is called "leverage."

37. D. The insurer has the right to approve (or disapprove) any assignment of the fire insurance policy. Coverage does not become effective until that assignment is approved by the insurer.

38. D. As long as the man owned his home for at least two years, lived in it as his primary residence and during the two year period ending on the date of the sale he has not excluded the gain of the sale of another residence, he is allowed to exclude any amount up to $250,000 of the gain from the sale of this property. Since he meets all these criteria and his gain is less than $250,000, the amount of capital gain is zero.

39. D. If the broker is mentally ill, it is up to the Commissioner to establish that fact and two outside witnesses would not automatically give the Commissioner the right to revoke the broker's license.

40. B. A fictitious person is someone that does not actually exist. Naming someone in a deed that does not actually exist would make the deed invalid and void.

41. B. When a casualty insurance policy is cancelled prior to expiration, the insurance company normally assigns a short-rate factor to the refund.

42. A. Not only must the trust fund records be balanced daily but, upon notice, the records must be made available to the Department of Real Estate for audit without further notice.

43. B. An attachment is a process by which real or personal property of a debtor is seized and held in custody of the law as security for the satisfaction of a judgment the creditor hopes to secure as the result of a law suit. The attachment creates a lien against the property and it may not be sold free of the attachment without satisfaction or release of the attachment, or the posting of a bond.

44. A. Equal right of possession is necessary in a tenancy in common; equal interest is not necessary. Unity of time or taking title at the same time is also not necessary, and neither is unity of title, nor being shown on the same document.

45. D. Only two of the answers indicate a partial or undivided interest in property. Joint tenancy has the right of survivorship tenancy in common does not.

46. C. $80,000 × 21.25% = $17,000 down payment. $80,000 − $17,000 = $63,000 loan. $63,000 × 10.25% = $6,457.50 interest per year. Interest: $6,457.50 divided by 12 = $538.13 per month. Taxes: $800 divided by 12 = $66.67 per month. Insurance: $978 divided by 36 = $27.17 per month. So, the first month's payment is $119.00 + $538.13 + $66.67 + $27.17 = $750.97.

47. C. A negative declaration is an indication that the proposed subdivision will have no adverse effect on the environment.

48. D. In California, non-resident applicants for real estate licenses must sign an additional agreement with the Department of Real Estate called a "Consent To Service Of Process." This agreement provides that should the need arise and the Commissioner be unable to locate the non-resident licensee using reasonable means, then service of the necessary legal papers on the Secretary of State in California will constitute service on the licensee and the legal action can proceed.

49. D. The most difficult step in the capitalization approach is to select the appropriate capitalization rate.

50. A. A turnkey project is a housing development in which a private contractor has completed the building to the point of readiness for occupancy. The development is then sold to the customer at a pre-arranged price. The dwelling is furnished.

51. B. Definition of studs. They are generally 2 inches by 4 inches by 8 feet, and are normally located 18 inches apart, measured from the center of each.

52. C. The Real Estate Commissioner must follow the Administrative Procedure Act by filing an accusation and then proceeding against the broker.

53. A. The purpose of a deed is to convey ownership of real property from the Grantor to the Grantee.

54. D. This process is known as down zoning because it usually reduces the economic value of the property involved.

55. C. In the attempt to provide full knowledge concerning the franchise, the law requires extensive disclosures to prospective franchisees prior to the signing of the contract to purchase. It does not protect stockholders or deal with territorial matters.

56. D. A Quitclaim Deed is a release of any and all, past or present, interests the grantor may have, but it does not contain any warranties and does not convey after-acquired title. To seize property means to take possession of it, and the grantor would certainly not take possession.

57. C. This is an example of leverage. Borrowing money at 6% interest and earning 8% interest on the investment enhances the equity yield.

58. B. The appraiser bases her appraisal on facts obtained from her survey and the result is her estimate as of a specific date. She cannot be expected to foresee what will happen tomorrow or in the future with regard to the value.

59. A. A life estate, because it is inheritable and of an indefinite duration and completely transferable, would be considered to be a freehold estate. The leasehold estate and estate for years would be less than freehold estates.

60. B. Under California law, a real estate salesperson is the employee of his/her broker and can receive compensation only through his/her employing broker. He/she can never collect commission directly from a principal.

61. D. A salesperson is considered as an employee of a broker since he is not licensed to act as an agent for another. Some salespeople sign an employment contract designating them as independent contractors, but they are still considered employees.

62. D. An agreement to perform an act that cannot be fully performed within one year from the date of the making of the agreement must be in writing to be enforceable. Though the agreement may be valid, because it was not in writing, it would be unenforceable in a court of law. Stock, trade fixtures and goodwill are personal property, and a verbal agreement may be used to employ the agent.

63. C. Conveying the title will alienate the title to property.

64. C. The Attorney General of the State of California acts as a consulting attorney to the Governor and all major office holders, including the Real Estate Commissioner.

65. C. Economic or social obsolescence concerns factors of the surrounding properties within the same geographic area, such as: are the tenants prospering or is it a depressed area, etc.

66. C. Leverage indicates the use of borrowed money so that the return can be maximized.

67. D. The Prepaid Rental Listing Service agent must keep proper records that are open for inspection by the Real Estate Commissioner. Such agents must account to their principals at least quarterly as to the disposition of such funds.

68. C. An attachment lien is good for three years and may be renewed.

69. C. A property described as a personal residence is considered adequate even if other properties are owned on the same street. However this would not be true if it were described as the owners "residential property." Residence (owner occupied) - Residential (property located in a residential area).

70. B. Such a situation would create a voidable contract; that is, it would give the seller the right to invalidate the contract because of the misrepresentation.

71. C. The capitalization rate indicates the return that the owner expects on the purchase price. The greater the risk involved in the investment, the greater the capitalization rate.

72. A. The price is always a credit for the seller and a debit for the buyer.

73. A. In appraising by the "cost" method, square footage is very important. In appraising by the "comparison" method, the comparisons used should be of the same approximate size (square footage).

74. B. The economic life of an improvement is the period of time in which it is economically productive.

75. B. A lender cannot give "kick backs" to real estate licensees for referring customers and clients. The real estate commissioner doesn't have any jurisdiction over banks, but he can discipline any licensee receiving any illegal "kick back" from a lender. The broker does not have to be disciplined because he notified the Real Estate Commission immediately and used reasonable supervision of his employed licensees.

76. C. The definition of property is rights or interests that a person has in the thing owned.

77. B. Surface waters are those waters not flowing in a defined channel. You cannot divert these to another's property if they will be a detriment to that individual's property.

78. B. Private restrictions placed by one grantor and affecting only one grantee would not be considered an overall great force.

79. D. The Preliminary Public Report would be invalidated by any of the ways listed in answers A, B, and C.

80. B. When the vesting is joint tenancy, each co-owner has a separate interest in a single title.

81. D. A loan-to-value ratio (LTV) describes the maximum amount a lender is willing to loan based on a percentage of the lender's appraised value of the property. For example, if the LTV ratio is 80%, this means that a lender may loan 80% of the property's appraised value to a borrower.

82. A. Under the terms of Article 7 of the Real Estate Law regarding junior loans of less than $10,000 - Maximum commission allowed on loans with payoff terms of less than two years is 5%, two years but less than three years is 10% and three years or more is 15%. In this example, at 15%, the commission on $4000 is $600.

83. A. Ownership in joint tenancy always includes the right of survivorship; hence, upon the death of Mrs. Layman, the property would pass to Mr. Layman automatically.

84. D. A valid land contract must be in writing as well as have the other four elements required on any contract. Those are consideration, consent (offer/acceptance), capacity and lawful object.

85. A. The prepayment penalty benefits the lender (the beneficiary). Should the borrower (Trustor) pay off the note in advance of the due date, the lender would receive an additional amount of cash over and above the balance due on the loan as a penalty charge to the borrower. This clause also benefits the lender in the event that the note is sold; the note is more desirable (more saleable) because of this clause.

86. A. Location is the most important factor influencing value.

87. A. The California Real Estate Law, along with laws governing other business and professions, is included in a section of the state Code of Regulations called the Business and Professions Code of the State of California.

88. C. The party required to report the sale of a single family residence is the RESPA settlement agent, escrow or the party who prepares the closing statement, usually the escrow holder.

89. C. This Federal Law, known as Interstate Lands Sales Full Disclosure Act, allows a seven day right of rescission.

90. B. The real estate agent's fiduciary obligation is to the seller. He does have the responsibility to reveal material facts to the buyer, but his loyalty and the fiduciary relationship is owed to the seller.

91. B. They are: Humboldt Base Line and Meridian, Mt. Diablo Base Line and Meridian, and San Bernardino Base Line and Meridian.

92. B. Fee means "an estate of inheritance." This is the highest and most common form of real property ownership in California.

93. B. A Bill of Sale transfers title to personal property in much the same way that a deed transfers title to real property.

94. A. Funds obtained through the Improvement Act of 1911 must be used to improve the property, including off-site improvements such as streets, sewers, etc., but not to purchase land.

95. A. Anything of value given to the buyer must be disclosed to all parties.

96. D. In an installment sale, the amount of an assumed loan which exceeds the seller's cost basis is treated as part of the down payment and is taxable in the year of the sale.

97. C. Maintenance expenses for one's own residence are not deductible.

98. B. An estate of inheritance is a fee simple estate. A fee simple estate by definition is of perpetual duration, capable of being conveyed during life or upon death.

99. D. The higher the EER, the greater the efficiency of the appliance.

100. B. Individuals under 18 years of age who are married are considered adults. A lease does not have to be signed by the wife.

101. B. The definition of capitalization is the process of expressing anticipated future benefits of ownership in dollars and discounting them to a present worth at a rate which is attracting purchase capital to similar investments.

102. C. An unlawful detainer action is a court action used by a lessor or owner of the property to oust a tenant who is there illegally.

103. D. The employment contract designating a salesman as an Independent Contractor has no bearing upon the salesman's obligation to work only through his employing broker, imposed by the Real Estate Law.

104. B. The statement of the question is a good definition of gross scheduled income.

105. B. The fact that another offer is coming in must be disclosed. This would be considered a material fact.

106. D. The buyer is a customer-prospect. The broker does not have a fiduciary/agency relationship with the buyer, but the law requires that a customer-prospect be treated fairly and honestly. It is the responsibility of an agent to divulge to a customer-prospect any information of a material nature that could affect the transaction. Since the broker failed to do so, he would be liable. Also, because he was representing the principal, the principal would have a course of legal action for misrepresentation by the broker.

107. D. While Brooks did not record his deed, he did occupy the property and apparently was in possession of it. Possession gives constructive notice, and therefore Carr's recording of his deed to the property would not create priority for his claim to be the owner.

108. D. Fruit and nut trees can be depreciated as property held for the production of income, trade or business. Owner occupied property as indicated in answers B and C, and raw land stated in answer A cannot be depreciated.

109. D. Real property, such as the purchase of a home, tend to increase in value in an inflationary economy and generally at a rate of value growth that exceeds the rate of inflation. Savings accounts tend to offer rates of return far below the inflation rates. Fixed interest rate government backed loans also tend to offer undesirable returns as would long term government bonds, which normally carry rates lower than that of other investment opportunities.

110. D. A franchise does not need to be registered with the Department of Corporations Commissioner if the net worth of the franchisor is more than $5,000,000.

111. B. Estimating the value of a property located at the intersection of two streets could be influenced by the fact that the merchant would be afforded more window display area and entrance from either street. This is called "corner influence."

112. A. Fee simple title is not necessarily free of loans or other encumbrances.

113. D. Since "O" retained a life estate when he sold the property to "A", he can do whatever he wishes with his interest. The sale of his life estate to "B" is permitted and "A" has no rights at this time to demand immediate possession.

114. C. Jed has a valid option. Although the consideration of $ 0.25 is small, it is sufficient. An option may extend for a period longer than one year.

115. A. When most of the mortgage lenders have substantial sums available for mortgage loans, they usually reduce their interest rate to attract borrowers from competing lenders. The other three business conditions mentioned in choices B, C, and D tend to drive rates up.

116. B. A real estate broker is allowed to handle an escrow without a special license, provided he or she had represented the buyer or seller in the original transaction. The law does not allow the broker to handle escrows under any other circumstances unless he or she forms a corporation and has it licensed as an escrow company.

117. C. Per the Rumford Act (California Fair Housing Act), ethnic information should not be revealed even if requested. This information is never considered a material fact.

118. C. Copies of the Structural Pest Control Report are sent by the Structural Pest Control Companies to the Structural Pest Control Board in Sacramento. The Board must keep copies of these reports for two years. They are then of public record and a copy of any report can be acquired by paying the required fee.

119. A. Of the items mentioned, the appraisal fee is the one that is not included in the finance charge.

120. C. The property held as collateral under the terms of the Deed of Trust secures the promissory note. A Trust Deed by itself has no value. It is the promissory note that is the negotiable instrument. A note cannot be recorded by itself. However, a Trust Deed can be recorded, which perfects the lien. If the Trust Deed is recorded, the note may be recorded along with it, as the Trust Deed secures the note.

121. B. The Ridge or Ridge Board is the highest point. The girder, collar beam and header are all parts found in wood frame buildings.

122. B. A broker who negotiates a sale while his license is in good standing has earned a commission and may collect it by proving that he was duly licensed at the time the sale was made, even though he was subsequently deprived of this license.

123. B. The husband or the wife is permitted to sign a contract for the sale of community real property, but the other spouse would have one year in which to void the sale. This makes the sale agreement voidable during that year.

124. B. A subdivider in 1930 may have placed a restriction that all homes must be at least $30,000 in value. This would be designed to protect all owners in the subdivision to see that adequate size homes would be built. With inflationary trends over the years, this limit would not have much benefit for those owners today.

125. B. It is considered deceptive advertising if the ad does not disclose that attendance is required to receive a prize.

126. B. Documentary transfer tax does not apply to an assumed loan, only to new money. New money is $20,000. $20,000 divided by $500 = 40. 40 × $.55 = $22.00.

127. B. The broker is entitled to no commission because this clause was not contained in the deposit receipt.

128. B. It would be the buyer who would assume the liability if no notice were published or recorded.

129. C. The best course of action available to the Commissioner would be a Desist and Refrain order. Such action would immediately halt all future sales for marketing of the property.

130. B. Accrued depreciation is the total of depreciation that has accumulated to date. A sinking fund refers to accrued income from an income property.

131. B. The key words are "should the contract later be defaulted" meaning it had been accepted. In the Standard Deposit Form, it specifies that if the buyer defaults, the broker is entitled to half the forfeited deposit but not to exceed the amount of commission contracted for, and only after the owner deducts any expenses for collecting the damages.

132. D. Conventional and FHA lenders may be paid their loan fees from anyone who agrees to pay for them. However FHA loans, being less risky, would have less points charged. VA (GI) limits the veteran to pay a maximum of reasonable and customary amounts for any or all of the "Itemized Fees and Charges" designated by VA, plus a 1 point charge by the lender, plus reasonable discount points. CAL-VET has a 1 point Loan Origination Fee (paid by the veteran) and like the VA, itemized reasonable and customary amounts for itemized fees and charges, plus reasonable mortgage broker fees.

133. A. Baker has an implied grant of an easement.

134. B. If the property dedicated to the city by the grantor is no longer used for the purposes granted (abandoning the easement), the original grantor may seek the return of that property to his possession. He could not, however, take the now public property through adverse possession.

135. D. Impound accounts are paid to the lender to build a fund of money so that they can pay the taxes and insurance when these large bills come due. It helps the beneficiary, in that the borrower does not default on the loan if they cannot make these payments, and it helps the borrower by making small contributions each month to cover a one major expense.

136. D. Because the amount is greater than $20,000 it does not come under the statues that govern Second Trust Deeds.

137. C. If a buyer does not have the money for a down payment or cannot qualify for adequate financing, he or she cannot buy a property although he or she may greatly desire to do so. Thus, the element of value known as "demand" is rendered ineffective by lack of purchasing power.

138. B. This would be a material fact that must be disclosed by the broker because the broker must treat all customer/prospects fairly and honestly.

139. B. This is referred to as a sandwich lease because there are three parties involved: the owner or landlord, the tenant, and the sublessor in the middle of the two.

140. B. A patio is a capital improvement and would be added to the cost basis on a residence. Insurance premiums are a cost of home ownership; interest on the loan is a tax deduction but does not affect the cost basis; depreciation can be taken on income, business or trade property, but not on residences.

141. C. If there is no provision, the escrow period is set at a reasonable amount of time.

142. C. The deed must have a property description but need not be acknowledged. Acknowledgement is done for recording, which is not necessary to the validity of the deed.

143. B. Although Impound Accounts are not mandatory on home loans, they are often used and they protect the lender and the borrower (trustor and beneficiary) by ensuring that your insurance and tax payments are made on time.

144. B. $400,000. market value. $335,000. trust deed unaffected by homestead exemption.
$65,000. equity of owner.
$100,000. homestead exemption (adequate to protect the owner's $65,000 equity).
Remember, the homestead exemptions are as follows:
$100,000 for head of household
$175,000 if the judgment debtor or spouse is 65 years of age or older or; 55 years of age or older with a low income unable to be employed due to a physical or mental disability
$75,000 for all others

145. B. The blood relationship of mother to son has no bearing on this situation. If a subdivider wishes to pay compensation to a person for selling homes in his/her subdivision, the law requires that the person he/she employs must have a real estate broker license.

146. C. The statute of limitations in California regarding encroachments is three years.

147. B. Proximity of an obnoxious nuisance is considered an example of economic obsolescence.

148. C. A tight money policy will cause a scarcity of money for financing. This usually means that there will be an increase of junior loans in real estate financing (Seller carrybacks).

149. D. Every exclusive listing must have a definite and final termination date according to the Real Estate Commissioner; a period of 24 hours is legal, because it has a termination date.

150. B. A township contains 36 Sections.

151. C. Tenants in Common hold a separate title to an undivided interest, which may be sold, willed, or encumbered separately without the consent of the other co-owners. Tenants in Common may own unequal interests.

152. D. There are no points on a Cal-Vet loan because the property is purchased outright by the Department of Veterans Affairs and then resold to the qualifying veteran with a land contract.

153. C. Advertising incentives are legal if proper disclosure is made to all interested parties.

154. B. Judgments are based upon common law and have been approved by statutes in California. Mechanics Lien rights were created by the legislature and do not derive from common law.

155. C. A judgment becomes a general lien on all non-exempt property in the county where it is recorded.

156. D. A well and pump would be considered man made improvements and are part of the owners title to the land.

157. C. In the rectangular survey system of land, a tier is defined as townships running north and south of a baseline.

158. D. The place where lenders sell existing loans to other lenders or investors is the secondary mortgage market. The Federal National Mortgage Association is the largest secondary mortgage market today.

159. B. Under eminent domain, the government may take private property for public use. However, "just compensation" is required under the U.S. and California Constitutions.

160. D. One holding a leasehold estate has a lease on the property and has a Chattel Real. In other words, a leasehold estate is considered personal property, not real property.

161. C. Mortgage companies often act as mortgage loan correspondents, helping insurance companies make loans to purchasers.

162. B. HUD must refer complaints to the enforcement agency of the state where the discriminatory housing practice occurred if HUD has certified that the agency has substantially equivalent laws, procedures, remedies and judicial review as federal law. Under a 1994 agreement reached with the California Department of Fair Housing and Employment (DFHE), the majority of discrimination complaints that HUD receives in California are referred to DFHE.

163. C. The owner of the servient tenement may take proper action to terminate the easement, but unilaterally revoking the easement by the servient tenement fails to terminate the easement.

164. C. An agreement of sale (land contract) gives the equitable owner the use of the property, as a lease gives the use of the premises to the lessee. An affiant (A) is one who makes an affirmation.

165. B. An attachment does not terminate upon the death of the defendant.

166. A. The principal could sue the agent if he or she is damaged by the lack of the agent's obedience to his or her instructions. The Real Estate Commissioner would be the one who would suspend or revoke his license, not a court.

167. D. Under regulations of the Alcoholic Control Board, no manufacturer's or wholesaler's license shall be issued to any person or premises to which a retailer's on-sale license is issued, and vice-versa.

168. D. Purpose of the Subdivision Law is to protect the public against fraud in the sale of such property. The location of the property is not the primary concern.

169. C. The contract is voidable, which means capable of being voided, but only by the innocent party, who in this case is the victim, Julie.

170. C. The word "waiver" as applied to a real estate transaction most nearly means a unilateral act and its legal consequences. One party "waives" certain rights.

171. C. The homestead exemption for a married person exempts $100,000 (subject to change) of equity from creditors.

172. D. Prescription relates to an easement, which is a real property right acquired through court action providing for the right to use the land of another.

173. B. Proper coverage is that which allows the property owner to be reimbursed for his or her losses.

174. B. The purchase price of the property is the basis for calculating depreciation. The fact that the previous owner had depreciated the property has no effect on the new buyer's cost basis.

175. D. Answer A suggests value in exchange. Answer B suggests value as an interpretation of future income in terms of present dollars. Answer C suggests value in use or inherent value. All of the following would be an accurate definition and useful information for an appraiser.

176. C. Insurance companies prefer to make large loans on commercial or industrial complexes. Banks, savings and loan associations, and mortgage companies are the more common sources of home loans.

177. A. Mortgage insurance premium is not a form of life insurance. It is a fund set up with money charged and collected from the borrower at the time the loan is made and paid to FHA. The money is then used to reimburse the lender in the event the borrower defaults on the loan.

178. A. The broker is liable to third parties for negligent and fraudulent misrepresentations. Material facts must be disclosed whether they are asked about or not.

179. D. The Federal Reserve Board may want to slow down the inflationary trend by any of these methods. Increasing the discount rate or the amount of reserves required for their member banks decreases the amount of money available for loans and consumer credit buying. Entering into the government bond market in a selling capacity will help them absorb some of the money in the economy so that it cannot be used for credit financing.

180. B. The Statute of Frauds states that certain contracts must be in writing. A general partnership does not have to be in writing; therefore, a partnership formed to invest real property does not have to be in writing. Be careful, because a partnership actually buying or selling real property must be in writing.

181. B. When title is held as community property it takes both spouses to convey title to that property. An agreement signed by only one spouse could not force the conveyance of that property.

182. C. Effective gross income is the term used to indicate the amount remaining after deducting vacancies from the gross income.

183. D. The provisions of the Rumford Act, which are found in the Health and Safety Code, now apply to all types of housing. The Act in its original form only applied to four or more units, but a law change 1978 extended the law to apply to all housing.

184. C. Commercial property must be depreciated over a period of 39 years.

185. C. Equity is the interest or value that an owner has in real estate over and above the liens against it.

186. C. Offering incentives to purchasers is legal, provided the seller and the prospective buyer are advised of the incentive and the seller agrees to the offer.

187. D. In a percentage lease, the rent is tied to a percentage of the gross receipts of a business.

188. C. "Call 1-800-For-A-Loan" is deceptive advertising because specific items will have to be verified after the phone call. Without regard to the content of the advertisement, all ads by a California Licensed Real Estate Broker negotiating loans for a borrower must include the Mortgage Broker's License Number.

189. B. A notice of non-responsibility would be used by an owner when improvements are ordered by someone else. The other steps are normal steps for a lender to take in ascertaining that his loan has first priority.

190. B. The probable selling price would be $600,000, since in most cases the seller would retire the assessment lien from the proceeds of the sale.

191. D. The activities described in the question are called blockbusting or panic selling and are definitely illegal. The licensee's conduct is definitely not legitimate, and a licensee could get into serious trouble for conducting business this way.

192. D. Depreciation is very important in the estimate of value using the replacement cost approach. The newer the building, the easier to determine the depreciation.

193. D. A Trust Deed is a piece of paper, movable and not attached to the land. Therefore, it is personal property.

194. B. This is a textbook definition of a holographic will.

195. C. Et ux is Latin for "and wife." Occasionally the term "et al" is also used on the state examination and it means "and others."

196. D. In an area where average-quality homes are being constructed among high-quality homes, there would tend to be a decrease in the overall neighborhood property values.

197. B. The best hedge against inflation would be an investment in an income-producing property that will maintain its value.

198. B. The old Abstract of Title was a search of the records together with a summary of all the pertinent records discovered in the search. It disclosed more than a Chain of Title or what is given in a preliminary title report, though it offered no guarantees as to its accuracy, as does Title Insurance.

199. D. California law allows a partnership to take title in any of the ways listed.

200. C. Delinquent interest on unsecured loans is not a proration item. All other items will be prorated at the close of escrow.

201. D. A Public Report is issued for a maximum of one year. However, it would terminate should the final Report be issued within that year or if any material change occurred where a new Public Report would have to be issued to replace the old Report.

202. B. An easement is not an estate in real property, but rather, it is a real property right.

203. B. The showing of homes is an activity restricted to a real estate licensee. In this case, the handy man is subject to a fine for performing such activity and receiving compensation without being licensed.

204. B. The trustee receives the bare or naked title (the right of conveyance), which creates the lien when the Deed of Trust is recorded. When the loan is paid in full, the beneficiary sends the trustee a request for reconveyance and then the Trustee reconveys the title back to the Trustor (borrower) through the issuance and recording of the deed of reconveyance. Should the loan go into default, then after the publication period, the Trustee would hold a Trustee's Sale and convey the title to the successful bidder.

205. B. Note that there is no uniform zoning symbol in California. However in most local governments in California the following symbols are used: R= residential such that R-1 = single family dwellings; R-2= duplexes; R-3= multiple family dwellings; R-4= high density multiple family dwellings; C= commercial; M= manufacturing; A = agricultural.

206. A. The money encumbrance or lien is placed on the property without the owner's consent and is therefore involuntary.

207. C. Describing land by fractional sections together with the township and range numbers is a legal description based on a U.S. government survey.

208. B. The title company will demand proof of emancipation to be sure that the grantor is competent to convey title.

209. D. A specific lien applies to a specific parcel of property. The other answers all include at least one general lien.

210. D. All points mentioned in choices A, B, and C would be considered misrepresentation by an agent.

211. B. A deed grants title under a real estate transaction; a Bill of Sale transfers title to personal property in a business opportunity transaction.

212. D. A statement prohibiting recording would not be enforceable in California; that is, the vendee (buyer) can always record a contract to protect himself.

213. B. Generally, title to personal property is transferred by a Bill of Sale or Transfer of Possession, e.g., a purchase from a vending machine is a transfer of ownership by a change of possession. Usually, there is no document placed in the public schools.

214. D. Section 10176(d) sets forth the penalty of a revocation or suspension of license for acting for more than one party in a transaction without the knowledge and consent of all parties involved in the transaction.

215. B. Liquidity refers to the cash position of a business; it would be best described by deducting the current liabilities from the current assets. The difference would reflect the cash available immediately.

216. A. Historically, commercial banks, savings and loan associations, and insurance companies have made real estate loans. There is an increasing shift of money from pension funds into real estate.

217. B. A prime tenant is a major tenant. All of the other choices would be considered major.

218. B. An affirmation is a verification or declaration that is not sworn to. An affidavit is a declaration reduced to writing that is then sworn to under oath.

219. D. A co-owner holding a tenancy in common interest in real property cannot obligate the other co-tenants for the whole property without their consent. The one co-tenant could enter into a lease for his or her interest in the property but not of the whole.

220. C. Borrower's need is usually the least important factor.

221. C. The original cost of a property, especially an old one, is the least important factor in determining its present value.

222. B. The loan broker law allows a maximum of 10% commission for negotiation junior loans in this amount to be paid off in two or more, but less than three years.

223. C. Because of the "amenity" nature of single-family residence property and the emotional appeal involved, the best analysis of current market value of such properties is by comparison.

224. A. The appraisal verified the value at $200 per acre, thus relieving the broker of any possible accusation of taking unfair advantage of the buyer.

225. D. With full employment and a high level of national production, people will be earning more money, which in turn will increase the demand for housing and the cost of homes.

226. C. By definition. Answer D omits the major city.

227. C. Use a listed price of $1,000,000.
　　$1,000,000 listed price − 20% = $800,000 purchase price.
　　$1,000,000 selling price − $800,000 = $200,000 profit.
　　$200,000 profit divided by $800,000 cost = 25%

228. D. Contracts that are to be performed in less than one year, such as a month-to-month rental, and agreements leading up to the final contract listing for a month-to-month rental) need not be in writing to be enforceable.

229. C. Joint tenancy requires the four equal unities of time, title, interest, and possession between two or more parties. Once any of the four unities is broken, it can no longer be a joint tenancy.

230. A. The cost approach cannot be used on vacant land.

231. C. Escrow instructions usually authorize escrow to call for the funding of the buyers loan. Escrow officers cannot make any changes to the escrow instructions or favor one party over the other. The escrow officer is a neutral third party, hired to simply carry out the escrow instructions.

232. B. Under an exchange agreement, the real estate licensee acts for both parties. This is one instance where he could earn a commission from each party to the transaction.

233. A. This type of construction financing is referred to as obligatory advances or fixed disbursement schedule.

234. D. Since the party died intestate they left no will and the distribution of the property is under the direction of the probate court according to the laws of intestate succession.

235. A. Any time you sign a note or sell a note and the amount you receive is less than the amount stated on the face of the note you are "discounting the note."

236. A. Choices B, C, and D are all methods of estimating the building cost; A is the method used to estimate value of vacant land.

237. D. An apartment building of five of more units converted to a condominium is not exempt under the Subdivided Lands Act, and a condominium conversion of two or more units is covered under the Subdivision Map Act and must be filed with local authorities.

238. C. When you consider the condominium units as well as the common areas, you have a condominium project.

239. B. The title policy would guarantee to the lender that there were no prior liens on the property. If any did arise at a later date, the title company would protect the lender at that time.

240. A. Wear and tear from use is physical deterioration. Out-of-date equipment is functional obsolescence. Change of locational demand and misplacement of improvement are both economic obsolescence.

241. C. Real estate investments are generally considered riskier than bonds or trust deeds and therefore should have a higher rate of return.

242. C. FHA insures loans with mutual mortgage insurance; it is used by FHA to pay lenders any loss within the insurance limits resulting from foreclosure.

243. C. The statement in answer C describes a "complete" escrow. Usually an escrow is "complete" in the evening and closes the following morning when the deed is recorded.

244. D. A tax shelter protects part of the owner's income or profits from taxation. The use of any of these techniques could lead to a tax savings.

245. A. CLTA Standard covers matters of public record, forgery and incompetency in the chain of title, and court defense costs to defend the title for the coverage given. Extended coverage would also include physical aspects that standard coverage does not. Neither policy covers losses caused by governmental regulations.

246. B. The Institute of Real Estate Management (IREM) recommends that property managers refrain from taking discounts or commissions arising out of purchases, contracts, or other expenditures of clients' funds, unless such income is fully disclosed to the property owner and accepted with his permission.

247. C. For example, if the purchaser has a judgment against him when he obtains the purchase-money mortgage, the purchase-money mortgage takes priority if there is a foreclosure or trustee's sale.

248. D. The contract would be signed "Mary Johnson" or it could also have read "Mary Johnson, a married woman" or "Mary Johnson as sole and separate property" depending on whether it is being purchased with community funds or separate money. The indication in the question is that it would be purchased as community property. A spouse buying in their name only indicates or implies community property should there be no indication of separate property.

249. C. Joint tenancy requires the four "unities" of time, title, interest, and possession (TTIP), combined with the right of survivorship.

250. A. Acknowledgment is only necessary if the deed is to be recorded. In writing, signed by the grantor and a competent grantor are all essentials to a valid deed.

251. B. The notice of non-responsibility serves notice to workers that the project was not ordered by the owner.

252. C. A deed may be valid without being dated or recorded.

253. D. Termination of an easement results from express release, which may be a Quitclaim Deed, signed by the holder of the dominant tenement, or by mutual agreement of the parties involved.

254. B. Zoning laws have been held by the courts to be a valid exercise of the police power of the city or county.

255. D. The lender is allowed to charge the seller the points to compensate the lender for charging a lower interest rate than he would otherwise charge.

256. C. A lease is an estate in the property of the landlord.

257. A. This symbol represents Equal Housing Opportunity.

258. A. Failure to place the name of the broker in an advertisement is referred to as Blind Advertising.

259. B. A real estate licensee is usually an agent and, as such, has a fiduciary relationship with his/her client.

260. C. A general partnership agreement need not be in writing whether it is dealing in real property or some other type of purchase.

261. B. Under the circumstances stated in the question, only represents an action that could be taken by a licensee. He may not accept an offer with a deposit until the final public report is issued, nor may he take an exclusive listing without a termination date under any circumstances, and he may neither lease nor sell the property until the final public report is issued.

262. B. A subdivider in 1930 may have placed a restriction that all homes must be at least $30,000 in value. This would be to protect all owners in the subdivision to see that adequate size homes would be built. With inflationary trends over the years, this limit would not have much benefit for those owners today.

263. A. The date of the purchase contract relates most to the value agreed upon by the buyer and seller.

264. A. An encumbrance is anything that affects or limits the fee simple title to or affects the condition or use of real estate.

265. D. Most courts would agree that the broker should have disclosed his interest in the investment company that was purchasing the property. The safest course for the broker in any event where there is a doubt is to disclose his and the salespersons' interests.

266. D. An important provision in the contract has been altered without the buyer's consent and he may, therefore, rescind the contract and recover all of his money. While Answer B is correct, Answer D is the more correct answer.

267. A. Most judgments may be appealed to a higher court. Therefore, a Lis Pendens applies throughout the period of court proceedings and would continue on through any appeal period. Once the judgment is final, the Lis Pendens no longer applies.

268. D. All are true statements about property. Property may be real or personal, a fixture or a lease.

269. C. Leaseholds are estates in real property; life estates imply an estate in remainder or reversion upon termination of the designated life. Estoppel refers to an easement that is not being used. Lenders, such as beneficiaries under a Deed of Trust, do not hold an estate in real property.

270. B. This case, Jones vs. Mayer, originated in the St. Louis, Missouri, courts and the Supreme Court decision was given in July 1968.

271. A. Dark colors make a room seem much smaller. This may not seem pertinent, however a savvy salesperson will be aware of the correct statements and use that knowledge to help him or her sell homes.

272. B. A mortgage assumed by the buyer would be charged against the seller's proceeds, since the seller had the obligation to pay off that mortgage. Such an entry would be recorded as a credit to the buyer against the purchase price, and a debit to the seller.

273. A. Statement of fact. The Real Estate Settlement Procedures Act is the law requiring lenders of federally related mortgage loans to make all necessary, required disclosures.

274. D. All of the above may be considered "boot" in a tax-free exchange.

275. C. On Junior Trust Deeds of less than $20,000 with a payoff period of three years or more, the licensee can collect up to a 15% commission.

276. C. A minor signing a contract has no competency and therefore would make the contract void. However, if the question had shown that the contract was signed while the person was a minor but that person is now an adult (18 years of age or older,) the contract would be voidable. A minor who signed a contract has a right to ratify the agreement when they obtain their majority age of 18 or older.

277. C. The notice must be published only once, but it must be published at least 12 days before the bulk transfer is to be commenced.

278. D. Private restrictions are limitations on the use of property by prior owners, including the subdivider/developer, and may be conveyed (i.e., transferred) by deed, by written agreement (i.e. contract), or included in the general plan restrictions, or developer's "Declaration of Restrictions" in subdivisions.

279. A. A judgment lien is an involuntary lien. If you placed a judgment lien on a person's property, he certainly would not have agreed to that lien.

280. A. Known as the Rumford Act, complaints under the Fair Housing Act should be taken to the Fair Employment Practices Commission (F.E.P.C.), a California governmental administrative agency housed in the Department of Industrial Relations.

281. A. The vast majority of junior money (loans other than first loans) is procured from private lenders or investors generally through the services of loan brokers (mortgage companies). Answer choices B and C are incorrect as banks and savings and loan associations generally make first priority loans, and only a very small amount of junior loans. Answer choice D is incorrect as credit unions can make both first and junior loans but are not currently a major source of these funds.

282. A. The right of survivorship is the main characteristic of a joint tenancy holding. Since either spouse may will part of his or her community property interest, the right of survivorship does not always exist under this holding.

283. A. The usual method of appraising income property is the capitalization of future net income. Inversely proportional economic life would not represent the value of an investment property. A gross multiplier factor plays a part in determining value, but is not the sole determinant.

284. D. For a land contract to be valid, it does need to be in writing. The other essential elements are consideration, legality, offer/acceptance and capacity. Instead of offer/acceptance, "mutual consent" could be used.

285. B. Growing crops are treated as personal property for purposes of financing. The security agreement is the document used to create a security interest in personal property. A trust deed, bill of sale and notice of sale do not fit the bill.

286. D. A license is the personal, revocable, non-assignable permission to do some act on the land of another. A ticket to a sports event is a license. An easement is assignable.

287. C. A power of attorney must be recorded if it is to be effective with regard to any real estate transactions by the attorney-in-fact.

288. C. As a city is a corporation, it would hold title in severalty.

289. A. Under an open listing, the broker that is the procuring cause is the one who earns the commission. It also allows the owner to sell the property himself or herself without paying a commission.

290. B. If an item sells for $1.00 and prices increase by 20%, this means that the same item will sell for $1.20. $.20 is 1/6 of the $1.20 price (.20 divided by 1.20 = 0.1666). This means that the price of the item has increased 16 2/3%, so the purchasing power of $1.00 has decreased by 16 2/3%.

291. A. 10% of 36 square miles (a township) = 3.6 square miles. One mile by one mile = 1 square mile. Two sections (1 square mile per section) = 2 square miles. 5280 feet (1 mile) by 5280 feet (1 mile) = 1 square mile.

292. B. Insurance companies are not regulated with respect to their real estate loans, and they are permitted to make the loan term as long as they wish. By custom we will find that they make shorter terms, but by law they could make the longest term.

293. C. Stock in a corporation is movable and, therefore, is personal property. (However, stock in a mutual water company is an appurtenance to the land. It benefits a specific property and is, therefore, real property.)

294. C. If the seller allowed the broker to represent him in dealings with third parties, the seller is responsible for all acts including any misrepresentations made by the broker. The creation of an agency relationship is not dependent upon a written contract. It is true, however, that a broker must have a written agreement in a suit for a commission.

295. B. All written instruments are personal property. Should they relate to an interest in real property, they would be also known as chattels real. Although a mortgage is both chattel real and personal property, not all lien instruments would be (example: a Security Agreement that holds only personal property as security for a loan). Mortgages do not create an estate in real property or less-than-freehold estates. They create liens only.

296. C. Only when a lease is made for more than one year must the spouse obtain the other spouse's consent. This lease is for exactly one year. Therefore, it is a valid and enforceable lease.

297. D. Economic life of an improvement depends on the owner's repair policy, use of the improvement, and the condition and age of the improvement.

298. C. The Uniform Commercial Code, Division 6, bulk transfer of business goods law is primarily for the protection of the business creditors.

299. C. Private lenders, such as those who take back a second trust deed when they sell their homes, supply most of the junior loans negotiated today.

300. C. A trust deed hypothecates real property as security for a loan. The loan is evidenced by a separate document, namely the promissory note. A grant deed conveys the property.

301. B. Due to the susceptibility of the loss of value of the dollar due to high inflation, it is wise for the investor to keep his money in a real property investment.

302. D. In addition to the coverage stated, matters of record, forgery, impersonation, lack of capacity, and defective delivery are covered in the extended coverage.

303. A. Any time two or more persons hold title to property together, they must hold an undivided interest (tenants in common). This means that if you own one-third of the property, you cannot designate which one-third of the property you own.

304. B. A "seasoned loan' is defined as a loan with a past record of good or prompt payments.

305. D. The Attorney General acts as the legal counsel for the Real Estate Commissioner and would be involved in any of the situations listed.

306. D. If a beneficiary refuses to execute a request for a full reconveyance within a period of 30 days, he is liable for damages and a penalty of $300.

307. B. The unemployment rate may only indirectly affect the level of mortgage interest rates.

308. C. Assessing the highest and best use is always the first step.

309. B. As the seller's agent, the broker owes his allegiance to that party. The fact that he withheld the information that he was also involved in the purchase would be a violation of his position of the trust and would probably give the seller a right to refuse payment of the commission.

310. B. It can be compounded daily, monthly, quarterly, annually, or using any other time period. Compound interest always pays more for each percentage point of original interest than does straight interest.

311. C. The fact that no two parcels of land are exactly alike (i.e., nonsubstitutable) is the primary basis for a court of law to enforce the legal doctrine of specific performance.

312. D. You cannot discriminate in the sale of housing based on race, color, creed or national origin anywhere in the United States of America.

313. D. Before any lots can be sold the report must be given to the customer, they must read it and the seller must obtain a signature from the customer verifying that they have received a copy of the report. The Subdivided Lands Law does not apply to standard subdivisions within the limits of a city if there is no common area.

314. B. The definition of amortization is liquidation of an obligation on an installment basis.

315. D. In the market data approach, the entire property appraised is compared to the sales prices of recently sold properties.

316. D. Convert $2,400 monthly income to annual income ($2,400 × 12 months = $28,800 annual income). Gross Rent Multiplier × Gross Income = Value GRM × GI = V). So, 10.72 × $28,800 = $308,736 Value.

317. D. For a broker to be entitled to a commission, he must have an active license, produce a ready, willing, and able buyer on the agreed upon terms, and show that he was the procuring cause (i.e., responsible for the consummation of the transaction).

318. A. When there are few transactions of similar properties, there is really nothing to compare.

319. A. The main benefit is that the mortgage insurance protects the lender in the event of a loss due to foreclosure. A lesser benefit is the ability to sell the loan to FNMA in the secondary money market.

320. D. When a tenant sub-leases his interest in a lease, the sub-lessee is only liable to the original lessee for the rent agreed upon, and has no responsibility to the owner of the property. The original lessee remains liable to the owner even if the sub-lessee does not pay.

321. B. In the market data approach the appraiser attempts to find comparable properties to the one he's appraising. The prices of these comparables indicate the value of the home being appraised. If a buyer can find another home at a better price they will substitute that one for the other home.

322. B. The entire idea behind the law is to tell a borrower how much they are paying in the way of financing charges and what it works out to be on an annual percentage rate.

323. D. While answer choices B and C apply to any real property, they are also advantages of income-producing property.

324. D. A quitclaim deed carries no warranties, expressed or implied.

325. B. The death of either party terminates an offer.

326. C. Liens in the form of taxes, assessments or loans may affect the value of the property but have little effect on the actual USE of the land.

327. C. The Civil Code makes it mandatory to list in the contract any encumbrances that exist on the property such as taxes, trust deeds, deed restrictions, etc. A formal legal description of the property must also be given.

328. B. The dictionary defines a megalopolis as an extensive, heavily populated, continuous urban area, including any number of cities.

329. D. It has been held under criminal law in California that a post-dated check is the equivalent of a promissory note, and that the maker's failure to pay is not a crime. A broker cannot justifiably accept a post-dated check as a deposit unless there is full disclosure of these facts to the seller.

330. C. An adverse decision on a petition for a variance by the Planning Commission may be appealed to the local City Council or the Board of Supervisors. If turned down by the local governing body, there is no appeal to the courts.

331. B. Title insurance promises the buyer that things are true; in a Warranty Deed, the seller promises that certain things are true. Insurance backed by a large company is better than the promise of a person.

332. D. Prices and rents most accurately reflect the expansion and contraction of available spaces to meet demand.

333. D. A homeowner can only deduct the property taxes, interest payments and a portion of any uninsured casualty losses.

334. B. Because Brown's former property and new property are both income property, he may negotiate a tax-free exchange, otherwise known as a 1031 Exchange. That is not true for Smith.

335. C. The activities described are characteristic of primary lenders.

336. D. A Real Estate Investment Trust is required, among other things, to have at least 100 investors or members.

337. D. A deed in lieu of foreclosure is usually not used when there are junior loans on a property. If used on a senior loan, the lender will have to assume any junior loans.

338. D. The phrase "Time is of the essence" means that the performance of any act under the contract shall take place on or before the date(s) indicated.

339. B. The statement of the question is a good definition of compound interest.

340. D. Any discount allowed on the purchase of supplies or other materials by the supplier belong to the owner, and the broker cannot take this money.

341. B. What is described in this question is different from a condominium project because in a condominium, there is separate ownership only of interior air space and not of individual lots. Make sure you know the distinctions between the different forms of ownership that fall within the subdivision law.

342. C. "Transfer," "convey," and "assign" are used interchangeably in a deed to mean "to grant." "Devise" is real estate left by will.

343. D. Kind of obvious, but wanted to make sure that you knew the meaning of fiduciary.

344. A. A "beneficiary statement" is a statement issued by a lender indicating the balance due on an existing loan as of the closing date of escrow.

345. A. The statement of the question is a good definition of the word "license."

346. B. The definition of flashing is the sheet metal that is used to protect a building from water seepage.

347. A. Under current laws an injured party may elect to file an action for a remedy with either a state or federal court. Discrimination is a "Personal Damage" which is CIVIL not CRIMINAL in nature.

348. C. Under the Bulk Sales Law in the Uniform Commercial Code, the buyer must publish a Notice of Intention of Bulk Transfer at least once in a newspaper of general circulation in the county where the transfer is to take place, record the notice at the county recorders' office, and notify by certified or registered mail the County Tax Collectors Office. This was created to protect the creditors' interest in any unpaid inventory.

349. B. Many owners take into account deferred maintenance, economic obsolescence and even an unsatisfactory floor plan. Those who manage their own property overlook the fact that their time is worth money and do not consider this an expense.

350. D. The fair housing laws prohibit discrimination based on either sex or race.

351. D. The broker must hold the check as instructed but must advise the seller regarding the conditions of the offer.

352. A. The County Board of Supervisors will establish the real property tax rate. The county tax assessor determines the assessed values of real property. The tax commissioner runs the Board of Equalization, which collects taxes for the state.

353. D. CLTA Standard (CLTA title policy) covers matters of public record, forgery and incompetency in the chain of title, and court defense costs to defend the title for the coverage given. Extended coverage (an ALTA title policy) would, as part of the coverage, include physical aspects that standard coverage does not. Neither policy will cover losses caused by governmental regulations, such as zoning.

354. D. Both parties are bound, making it bilateral. Executory indicates that the contract is yet to be performed.

355. C. A percentage lease is based upon the gross sales with a minimum rental.

356. A. Prizes are not prohibited provided the advertisement specifically states that the award requires the attendance of the sales presentation.

357. C. A restriction is a limitation on the use of property. If a restriction in a deed is broken, the legal step for enforcement would be to get a court injunction preventing the violation from continuing.

358. C. Any agreement to assume someone else's debt must be in writing.

359. B. Cracks in the foundation and doors and windows not closing properly may result from settling. A soil engineer's report should be ordered to determine if there is a soil compaction problem.

360. B. Of the choices given, only answer choice B would confer (1) the right of survivorship together with (2) an undivided one-half interest; the former being a distinguishing characteristic of joint tenancy.

361. A. If the lease prohibits an assignment but the lessee assigns the lease anyway, the lessor has the right to void that assignment, making it voidable. Also, it does not immediately cancel the lease; it makes the lease a voidable lease.

362. A. A beneficiary statement is a lienholder's statement as to the unpaid balance on a trust deed note.

363. A. Highest and best refers to what will bring the highest net return over a given period of time. It is the starting point for appraisal.

364. C. $10.20 × 1,500 sq. ft. = $15,300.00. $3.25 × 216 sq. ft. = $702.00. Cost to construct in 1999 = $15,300 + $702 = $16,002.00. Since the property is 10 years old and the economic life is 50 years, the depreciation amount to subtract is 20% of $16,002, so depreciation (20%) = $16,002 × 0.20 = $3,200.40. Depreciated value of entire property = [$16,002 − $3,200.40 = $12,801.60 (improvements)] + $1,500.00 (land) = $14,301.60.

365. C. The most accurate appraisal would be one in which the appraiser could use all the approaches to correlate the value.

366. B. You should know the formula: Gross Multiplier × Gross Income = Value (GM × GI = V). You have to solve for the gross Multiplier at $690 income, then multiply the gross Multiplier by $600 to find the new value. You know that 2 × 4 = 8. If you substitute the numbers for the letters this means that Gross Multiplier is equivalent to 2. To get 2 you have to divide 8 by 4. Now solve for Gross Multiplier using the formula 2 = 8 / 4 (GM = V / GI). GM = $78,000 / $690. GM = 113.04347. Now solve for value with a GM of 113.04347 and GI of $600. GM × GI = V or 113.04347 × $600 = $67,826.08.

367. A. The State Board of Equalization collects the sales tax. It is due on the transfer of furniture and fixtures. Stock-in-trade and goodwill transferred are not taxable items.

368. B. A recorded judgment provides constructive notice.

369. B. Mortgage companies are used as loan correspondents by the life insurance companies. In this way the insurance company is relieved of the burden of originating and processing loans, as well as some administrative and service functions.

370. C. The word "blanket" indicates that the encumbrance "covers" more than one parcel of land. A blanket encumbrance is often used in financing a subdivision trust deed "covering all of the lots in the subdivision."

371. B. Debits on the closing statement are charges to the seller or buyer. In this instance, the seller has collected rents in advance and these rents will have to be turned over to the purchaser of the property. This requires a charge or debit against the seller's account.

372. A. There are a limited number of houses and rental units in a given area. The housing supply and demand in that area will directly affect the vacancy rate of apartments.

373. B. The Subdivision Law defines condominiums and apartment projects as subdivisions if they contain five or more units.

374. A. Article 7 indicates that the maximum term of an exclusive listing to negotiate a loan of $2,000 or less is 45 days.

375. B. This is considered a blind ad as nothing in the ad indicates that an agent is involved. The ad must contain the word "broker" or "agent" or the abbreviations "bro" or "agt."

376. B. Institutional lenders only include insurance companies, savings and loans and commercial banks.

377. D. The property belongs to the seller until the sale closes. The seller would have to give permission for the buyer to move in, and the permission should be in writing for the protection of all parties.

378. A. There is no contract and the offeror may withdraw or cancel the offer without a reason unless three things happen: (1) the offeror makes an offer; (2) the offer is received by the offeree and accepted; (3) the offeree's acceptance must be communicated back to the offeror.

379. D. The Note is the evidence of the debt and the Trust Deed is only incidental to it.

380. D. The answer choices A, B, and C are all important factors a lender considers when granting a loan approval.

381. A. The contract would not be binding unless acceptance had been communicated back to the buyer prior to death. The contract is void because it lacks mutual consent.

382. D. Mechanics Liens date back to the first day of construction.

383. C. This provision appears in the National Association of Realtor's (NAR) Code of Ethics.

384. A. Credit unions place a greater percentage of their funds into real estate loans. Credit unions have pretty much taken over the home loan market now that most savings and loans are no longer in business. These loans, namely, are in the single-family dwelling area. As for life insurance companies, they prefer long-term, higher-valued commercial properties. Commercial banks, due to the liquidity requirements, prefer short-term loans such as construction loans, although here too, funds are available for the home loan market.

385. A. If the sellers prepaid the taxes, they would expect to get the unused portion back, which will be a credit. The seller usually pays for title insurance and delinquent assessment liens. The assumed loan is a debit to the seller.

386. C. One of the requirements for a zoning ordinance to be considered lawful is that it promotes the general health, safety and welfare of the community.

387. B. As there would be no will (intestate) to designate the disposition of the estate, the heirs would be allowed by California Law five years to make their claims to the property. Should no heirs lay their claims within the designated time, the property would ESCHEAT to the state of California.

388. C. The only choice used to calculate net income is vacancy allowance.

389. A. The County Board of Supervisors annually sets the county tax rate.

390. D. As the depth increases, the front foot value increases. This is based on the 4-3-2-1 rule, stating that 40% of the value of property is in the front 1/4 of the lot, 30% in the next 1/4, 20% in the following 1/4 of the lot and finally 10% of the value of the property is in the rear 1/4 of the lot.

391. B. The major function of FHA was to create loans for home purchasers. This has been provided for under Title II of the law.

392. D. This is the definition of Gross National Product.

393. C. Crawl space must be at least 18 inches. This is the distance from the ground to the bottom of the floor joists.

394. C. An easement created by prescription can be terminated by non-use for a continuous period of five years.

395. D. HUD provides financial and technical assistance to local housing, including the rental markets and rates.

396. A. Change of flight patterns will cause property to lose value due to an outside cause, or the airplanes activity. This is also referred to as external or environmental obsolescence.

397. D. There are two parties to a Grant Deed. One is the grantor, who owns the property and is deeding it to another. The other is the grantee, who receives the deed and thereby, title to the property.

398. C. A major benefit of a limited partnership is that the limited partners will limit their liability to the amount of money they have invested or pledged to the partnership.

399. A. The best appraisal methods would be the Replacement Cost approach and the Capitalization of the Net Income approach. The Gross rent multiplier could be inaccurate and there would probably be very few shopping center sales for which you could use the Market Data approach.

400. C. A basic rule of economics is that land is necessary for the production of anything.

401. C. Quantity survey is the most accurate, but also the most detailed and difficult method of determining the cost of replacing an improvement at current cost. It requires a thorough itemization of all construction costs, both direct (such as materials and labor) and indirect (such as taxes, permits and insurance). Every material, labor, and indirect cost is estimated separately, and the individual costs are totaled. The quantity survey method can be used only by someone familiar with all facets of building construction.

402. B. The security for the debt is the title to the property held by the one joint tenant. If this one tenant were to die, the title would pass immediately to the survivor and the lender would no longer have any security for their debt.

403. B. One of the definitions of collateral from the dictionary is "property deposited as security, additional to one's personal obligation." In this instance a borrower used another note to secure the payment of his personal note.

404. B. VA (GI) home loans are made only to veterans who intend to occupy the property as a home. While the veteran must intend to occupy the home at the time of securing the loan, he can, after living in it, move out and rent the property without affecting the loan.

405. B. The "gross multiplier" assumes a correlation between market value and total gross income.

406. A. In an attempt to dispose of his assets so that they cannot be attached by creditors, a person will sometimes convey real property by a Gift Deed. The law protects his creditors against such subterfuge, and they can have the Gift Deed set aside in court.

407. D. Subornation has to do with entering into a conspiracy to commit perjury. The term has nothing to do with agency. The other choices suggest ways in which an agency can be created.

408. A. Under Cal-Vet financing, the interest rate may fluctuate during the term of the loan. If the interest rate is increased, the borrower has the privilege of keeping the payment at the same amount each month and therefore the loan term would be extended to the entire loan payoff.

409. D. In this situation, the broker is not acting in the capacity of an agent but as a principal and should advise the purchaser of his or her position.

410. A. FHA insures new loans, which may be sold on the secondary money market.

411. C. A homeowner is allowed to deduct interest payments, property taxes, and uninsured casualty losses for his primary residence each year, on his federal income tax return.

412. B. Only the neighbor could be sued. The broker, the Real Estate Commissioner, and the standard policy of title insurance would have no liability.

413. D. The Prepaid Rental Listing Service Agent must keep proper records that are open for inspection by the Real Estate Commissioner. Such agents must account to their principals at least quarterly as to the disposition of such funds.

414. B. Lee will pay off the existing loan which is most likely secured by a Deed of Trust. Upon payment in full, a deed of reconveyance would be issued to Lee, which when recorded would release the lien. If Gary paid all cash there would be no trust deed as there would be no lien created. A Bill of Sale is used to convey personal property, and therefore it would not be involved in this situation.

415. C. Deferred maintenance refers to physical deterioration of a structure, not the lack or amenities.

416. C. A hip roof has four sloping sides.

417. D. The Loan Broker Law requires, among other things, that the Broker's Loan Statement contain estimated costs, including appraisal, escrow, title, notary, recording and credit investigation.

418. A. It is impractical to place the restrictions in each deed since there are usually a great number of restrictions. It is better to record the restrictions and make reference to them in each deed.

419. A. The deposit belongs to the seller, once the conditions of the deposit receipt have been fulfilled.

420. A. An institutional lender is more likely to advance funds towards the purchase of a home. The Federal Housing Administration and the Federal Reserve Bank are not lenders in the home loan market.

421. A. The Principle of Substitution says that the value of a property tends to be set by the cost of acquiring an equally desirable substitute property.

422. A. A high Energy Efficiency Rating means that the air conditioner is more efficient, costing less to operate.

423. C. The IRS says that in order to qualify for a tax-free exchange, "like for like" properties must be exchanged; that is, property given and property received must be either income for income, investment for investment, trade for trade, or business for business property.

424. C. Essentials to acquire an Easement by Prescription: Continual use for five years, Open and Notorious use, Hostile to the true owner, Claim of right/color of title. NOTE: Payment of property taxes would be an additional element that would be necessary if attempting to acquire ownership through adverse possession; however, it is not necessary to obtain an easement.

425. A. The appraiser is concerned with the loss due up to this point. He or she is not concerned with the remaining life or actual age of the property, but with its effective age. He or she looks to the productive life of the property and considers how much of this has been used up.

426. A. The statement of the question is a good definition of the word "license."

427. C. It is perfectly acceptable for the salesperson to accept a personal note as a deposit, but this must be disclosed to the seller before the acceptance of the offer.

428. D. The lender would consider all aspects of the loan as mentioned in answers A, B, and C.

429. D. Desk cost is the total cost of operating expenses of an office divided by the number of desks in the real estate office.

430. B. Most houses are torn down before they fall down. When a house cannot be used for rental income or residential purposes it no longer has any economic worth and is generally torn down.

431. B. Even though an owner sells a property "as is" they still must disclose known defects, and must provide the buyer with a Disclosure Statement.

432. A. Stock in a mutual water company is an appurtenance. Each share is considered to be appurtenant to a specific piece of real property and cannot be sold separately. An appurtenance is defined as real property.

433. D. Such activity is described as both Panic Peddling and Blockbusting. Both of these activities are illegal and broker Coogan could face disciplinary actions should he decide to continue this conduct.

434. B. On the death of one joint tenant, the survivors take title to the property without the obligation to pay any unforeclosed liens.

435. B. Under the subordination clause, the beneficiary (holder of the note) allows the borrower to obtain additional financing at a later date with this later financing having first priority.

436. A. Joists are the beams that run horizontal and parallel to each other and are used to support the floor and ceiling loads. Joists are "beams" not "rafters."

437. D. A listing agreement that contains an option to purchase is first of all a contract employing the broker to act as an agent for the owner in the sale of the property, and that is her main role. If she exercises the option, she operates in the capacity of a principal in its resale, but this is secondary to her responsibility as an agent. Any time a broker takes a listing with an option to purchase, it must be disclosed to all parties involved.

438. A. Under the community property law, either spouse may will his or her one-half interest. The son, Thomas, would, therefore, inherit all of his father's interest - an undivided one-half.

439. C. The Commissioner's Final Subdivision Report expires five years from the date of issuance of the report or until there is a material change. In the event there is a change, this information should be reported to the real estate commissioner so an amendment to the original report can be issued.

440. C. Both subdivision laws stipulate that a division of land into five or more parcels to be sold, leased, or financed now or in the future, constitutes a subdivision.

441. D. For a broker licensee to use an ad that gives the impression that the property is being sold by the owner himself/herself when the broker has, in fact, secured a listing on the property, would constitute substantial misrepresentation. This kind of action is unlawful.

442. D. In arriving at the final estimate of value, an appraiser may use one or a combination of all three of the major approaches to appraising. It is the appraiser's responsibility to explain which approaches were or were not used and to explain the reason for using the approach the appraiser believed to be the most appropriate.

443. A. These second trust deeds are classified as promotional notes and are real property securities. The contractor must obtain a permit to sell them and since he is handling eight in one calendar year he is considered to be "in the business" and must have a license to sell them through a licensee. A dealer's endorsement is not required.

444. D. All personal service contracts, such as listings, are terminated immediately upon the death of either party.

445. B. Of the choices given, only the airspace above the land is considered real property.

446. B. The deadline for filing a Veteran's Exemption is April 15.

447. C. Under a real estate option only one party is bound by the contract. The optionee has the right to either purchase or not purchase and we consider this as being no mutuality in obligations.

448. C. The accusation must be filed within three years of the occurrence of the act that is considered grounds for revocation or suspension of the license.

449. B. Should any prospective purchaser enter your office requesting to see a particular property, you would assume they were interested in that particular property.

450. A. Disclosure statements required by RESPA must be provided the borrower at no cost.

451. D. All of the statements are statement of fact.

452. C. Zoning laws are an exercise of the police powers that are for the public health, safety, morals, and general welfare. No compensation need be paid in exercise of police power, as they are for public protection.

453. C. Since both buyer and seller agreed to the liquidated damages, the seller has agreed that if the buyer defaults, his sole claim will be to the $500.

454. D. A trust deed is not a contract, but rather is a conveyance of the naked legal title with the power of sale from the trustor to the trustee. Therefore, the trustee retains the right to sell the property under the trust deed at any time for the benefit of the beneficiary. The conveyance has been performed and therefore is not under the Statute of Limitations; hence, it never "outlaws."

455. A. An option to renew a lease is a promise by the lessor to do so in the event the lessee desires it. A promise in a contract is also known as a "covenant."

456. D. Upon request, the lender must allow the borrower to inspect the Uniform Settlement Statement one day prior to the close of the transaction, but the statement must be delivered only at or before the date of settlement (close of escrow).

457. C. The recommended process is for the lender to contact FHA for a "conditional" commitment; that is, for advance assurance that an FHA loan will be made, establishing the loan value for the house.

458. B. The surface of the earth and the material beneath the surface to the center of the earth is a part of real property. Since the airways are now public domain, the ownership of airspace is "use to an enjoyable and reasonable height."

459. C. The provisions of the Bulk Sales Law are found in the Uniform Commercial Code.

460. A. As discrimination is not a criminal act, we could eliminate answers (C) and (D). (B) is incorrect as the remedy available to the injured party is not limited to only action through a state court. It could take place through the federal courts.

461. D. All three choices refer to the lessee's interest in real property. Always keep in mind that a lessee's interest is personal property known as Chattel Real. The lessee describes a person who is renting property.

462. D. The statute of limitations allows four years during which action may be taken on any contract, obligation or liability founded upon an instrument in writing. Since a deposit receipt is a written agreement of this nature, action to enforce collection of commission must be taken within this time limit.

463. C. The Structural Pest Control Companies send copies of the reports to the Structural Pest Control Board.

464. A. Under any type of ownership, each owner has an equal right of possession. This means that any owner can go anywhere on the property regardless of the percentage of their overall interest.

465. A. Capitalization of income is a method of establishing the value of income type properties.

466. C. All sales staff members employed by a licensed real estate corporation must have some form of a license, either a salesperson or a broker.

467. C. By law, anyone other than the broker, such as a clerical employee, must be bonded in order to be able to withdraw funds from the trust account.

468. C. Definition of Riparian Rights: the rights of a landowner whose land touches a river or stream to use a reasonably appropriate amount of water as needed.

469. C. In appraising income property, it is necessary to know the net income of the property in order to use the capitalization approach. Such net income is calculated by subtracting from the gross income nearly all expenses except the debt service.

470. A. The Statute of Frauds is the California law that spells out which contracts must be in writing if they are to be enforceable in court. Commission splits are not included in the Statute of Frauds.

471. B. Adverse use of the property must be done openly and notoriously against the will of the owner, but this does not mean a public confrontation.

472. C. If two reports were issued and a report was required as part of the terms of the purchase agreement, both reports must be given to both the buyer and the seller by the escrow officer.

473. B. An appraisal must be made on the property, but this is not done by FHA.

474. B. Appurtenant easements "run with the land" and automatically pass to future grantees, whether mentioned in the deed or not.

475. B. Electrical wiring is placed inside a metal pipe called a conduit.

476. D. A recorded land contract shows an equitable interest in the property. When the vendee (buyer) defaults and abandons the property, the land contract becomes a "cloud on the title" until it is removed by either a Quitclaim Deed or Quiet Title action.

477. B. The existence of a better offer that is imminent could very well be a material fact to the seller. It would probably influence his decision concerning a present offer.

478. C. Location is the most important factor influencing value, the other factors being utility, size, shape, thoroughfare conditions, exposure, character of the business climate, plottage or assemblage, character of the soil, grades, obsolescence, building restrictions and zones.

479. B. Trade fixtures are considered personal property and would not be an appurtenance.

480. D. The cost method requires the determination of replacing the improvements "new" at today's costs of labor and material, then adjusting the "new" estimate downward by estimated accrued depreciation.

481. D. Inasmuch as the terms of the option are for all cash consideration and no unsecured promissory note is involved, it must be sold or assigned. Because the new holder exercised the option within the 60-day period (before July 30) and planned to purchase the property within 30 days of the exercise date (before August 30, the option is valid.

482. C. Marketability and acceptability of the property would be most important in determining its potential value to a buyer.

483. C. Both the principal's and agent's names must appear on an agreement signed under the provisions of a valid power of attorney. The principal's name would be written in and the "attorney in facts" name would be signed (signature necessary).

484. D. $345,000 is 9% more than the original cost.
> Add 9% to 100% to get 109%.
> Write a formula.
> 109% of Original Cost = $345,000
> Divide both sides of the formula by 109%
> 109% of Original Cost / 109% = $345,000 / 109%
> Original Cost = $345,000 / 109%. Original Cost = $316,513.76

485. B. Partners have personal liability in the partnership for the debts related to the business incurred by themselves and/or other partners. (A) Only corporate assets are held accountable. (C) Limited partners are limited in liability to their investment. Personal assets are not held accountable for debts of the partnership. The general partner holds all of the personal liabilities for the debts of the Limited Partnership.

486. B. If there is no will, separate property is divided one-half to the wife and one-half to an only child; or one-third to the wife and two-thirds to more than one child.

487. C. The taxpayer may pay all or part of the assessment bill within 30 days of receipt. Any amount left unpaid will then automatically go to bond and be payable in installments with interest, with the annual tax bill.

488. B. Fees for title insurance and escrow services are set by the Title Insurance Companies.

489. C. Seller must accept the agreement as presented. If he makes any change in the terms, no matter how small, it creates a counter-offer subject to acceptance or rejection by the buyer.

490. D. Statement of fact. One mile = 5,280 feet, 1/4 of that = 1,320.

491. A. Since there was a contingency clause, the buyer is relieved of his agreement to buy, and can demand return of the deposit.
Classification = Contracts 7

492. B. This is a clear example of a discounted note. Leveraging is the act of borrowing other's money (OPM) to finance the purchase of property. The more borrowed, the greater the leverage. Selling a note for less than the money owed is not illegal nor is it usurious (charging more interest than the legal rate allowed) as there is no mention of the interest rate being charged.

493. B. Some expenses would be less. There would be a smaller roof and foundation.

494. A. Appropriation is the giving of certain rights by a governmental or judicial body. Percolation is the ability of the soil to absorb and drain water. Eminent Domain is the right of the State to take property for public use. Estoppel is a principle of law that bars people from asserting certain rights.

495. C. All sales through the Probate Court must be approved by that court. The manner in which the sale is conducted is not specified in the Probate Code.

496. D. Probate distributes the assets of a deceased person; Escheat refers to property reverting to the state when a person dies leaving no heirs and no will.

497. C. Buyers and borrowers almost without exception acquire for their own financial protection a CLTA Standard Coverage Policy of Title Insurance. This gives them the protection normally needed and is less costly than CLTA Extended or ALTA Lenders Policy or Homeowners Policy.

498. B. Adjustable Rate Mortgages vary with the index to which they are tied.

499. A. A franchiser who has a net worth of at least $5 million is exempt from the Franchise Law in California.

500. D. The most current data or best way to assess property is to see what other, similar properties have been sold for, and use that as a base to begin the appraisal process. Classification = Valuation and Market Analysis 3

501. B. A licensee must reveal all material facts. A material fact is one that is likely to influence the principal's decision, such as massive plumbing repairs, or any defect of which the agent has knowledge or which is not apparent to a reasonable, prudent person.

502. C. Advising the owner to do anything would be condoning his attempt at discrimination. The broker should simply refuse to take the listing.

503. A. As the depth of the lot increases, the front foot value increases. Classification = Valuation and Market Analysis 3

504. C. Usury is defined as a conscious taking by a lender of more than the maximum amount of interest as allowed by law.

505. D. All of the items listed in choices A, B, and C are considered to be appurtenant to the land.

506. B. This is the definition of police power. Eminent Domain would refer to the process by which property is taken from private ownership to benefit the general public.

507. C. Mechanic's Liens are specifically exempted from the protection afforded by a declaration of homestead, whether filed before or after the homestead was declared.

508. A. The mortgage insurance protects the lender in the event of a loss due to foreclosure. Although the lender can sell the loan to FNMA, a secondary money market, it is not the main advantage.

509. C. The city can pass new zoning laws, but they cannot make these new ordinances apply to property that has been improved some years back. The laws cannot be retroactive.

510. D. Title insurance does not normally cover governmental regulations such as zoning matters.

511. D. This is a definition of capitalization.

512. C. Arbitration, if it is to be binding, must be agreed to by all of the parties. If there is a disagreement, the remedies open to the tenant include relinquishment of his rights or suing to enforce them.

513. C. This is the proper procedure when dealing with property owned by an unincorporated group.

514. B. The parties have agreed to liquidated damages by initialing an agreement to the effect that seller shall retain the deposit as his sole right to damages in event of default on the part of the buyer. This agreement about damages does not take away the seller's other remedy, which is a suit against the buyer for specific performance.

515. C. Less-than-freehold estates refer to leases and these are owned by the lessee. The landlord or owner has a freehold estate, and the lessee has the less-than-freehold estate.

516. C. The constitutionality of all fair housing laws is based upon the Thirteenth Amendment to the United States Constitution.

517. B. An appurtenant easement is a right to use another's land that is attached to the land. When this land is sold, this interest or easement passes to the grantee.

518. B. Mortgage payments may not be included in arriving at the adjusted cost basis; the choices are tax-approved adjustments.

519. D. Loss in the sale of a residence is not deductible.

520. D. A party that takes an option on property is under no obligation to disclose to the optionor what they intend to do with the property after exercising the option. The only time the optionee would be required to disclose anything is if that person were a licensee or the agent of the optionor. In this instance the original seller can do nothing.

521. B. Governmental bodies may control the use of private property in an effort to provide for the health, safety, morals, and common welfare of the community. Such authority is police power, which is the broadest power of the government to regulate and control private property.

522. B. The secondary mortgage market (or money market) is described as where loans are bought and sold by lenders (mortgagees). Answer choice A leads you to believe they are discussing the second priority mortgage loans. In answer choice C you would have to recognize that a mortgagor is a borrower. Answer choice D is the definition of the primary money or primary mortgage market.

523. D. This is a good definition of a life estate.

524. A. If he does not pay for the assessment in full within 30 days after completion of the work, the state will sell bonds to pay for the work and the owner of the lot may pay off the debt over a ten-year period.

525. B. The income approach is used on income properties, and this method would not apply to residences in a new subdivision, since these properties are generally not purchased for rental income.

526. C. If you add something to a printed form, it takes precedence over the printed matter.

527. B. According to the Subdivided Lands Act (Real Estate Law), all material changes regarding a subdivision approved by the Department of Real Estate must be reported to the Real Estate Commissioner immediately. The sale or optioning of five or more parcels to one purchaser in a subdivision is considered a material change.

528. B. Owner-occupied areas historically have a lower rate of turnover than non-owner-occupied areas.

529. A. A lease is an estate for years, which is a type of less-than-freehold estate.

530. B. Alienation is the act of conveying the title of real property to another. The opposite of conveyance is acquisition.

531. A. A person that grants, leases or hires real property is a tenant. The term "hire" would indicate a lease or rental.

532. C. The discrimination in housing provisions of the government specify that the renting or leasing to a roomer or a boarder in a single-family house that is unencumbered, provided that no more than one roomer or boarder is to live within the household, is exempt from the application of discrimination laws.

533. B. A prepayment penalty benefits the lender in that if the borrower pays off the loan in advance, he must pay a penalty to the lender because the lender did not expect to receive the money so soon, and, as a result, may have to reinvest the funds at a lower interest rate.

534. C. $ 72,000 × 2 = $144,000 Sales Price.
    $ 72,000 minus $20,000 = $52,000 loan
    $144,000 − $52,000 = $92,000 made
    $ 92,000 / $20,000 investment = $4.60

535. B. There is no right of survivorship with tenancy-in-common. Therefore, when a co-tenant dies, his or her share passes to those named in that person's will (devisees) or to that person's heirs.

536. A. A lease is not affected by the transfer of the title to the property.

537. B. In making adjustments for differences in properties, the comparables are adjusted to the characteristics of the subject property, because the comparables are given and the subject property value is unknown.

538. B. Real estate law requires a licensee to disclose to his principal all facts known by him/her pertaining to a transaction. Such disclosure is also required by the laws of agency. Therefore, if a licensee can save his principal $6,000 by informing him that his loan can be paid off at a 50% discount prior to the sale of the property, he must inform him of that fact.

539. D. Answer choices A, B, and C all relate to the alternatives the buyers would have if they should not acquire the 100% financing. The key to this problem is the contingency clause, which allows the buyers to be released from the contractual obligations if the contingency is not met within the time specified in the agreement. The question showed no time limit. However, the contract was based on the 100% financing, which could not be obtained by the buyers.

540. B. Such an omission would not invalidate the deposit receipt.

541. D. All of the above: an Attachment Lien holds the property for a pending judgment; a Subpoena calls for an appearance at a court hearing; and a Lis Pendens notice is recorded to notify the public of pending litigation of the property.

542. D. There are five "tests" of a fixture, and the cost item is not one of them. The five tests are: method of attachment, adaptability of the item, relationship of the parties, intention of the parties, and agreement between the parties.

543. A. An Abstract is a summary or digest of information; hence, the summary concerning the Chain of Title is known as an Abstract of Title.

544. B. A "cloud of title" is often the result of another's potential claim to all or part of the title. Such a "cloud" is most easily removed by the claiming party withdrawing the claim. The Quitclaim Deed is the document used. Under a Quitclaim Deed, the grantor grants only the interest that the grantor has at the time the conveyance is executed.

545. B. The Dominant Tenement is an owner who has an easement over another person's land, known as a Servient Tenement.

546. C. A blanket encumbrance is a general lien on many properties; real property tax is a specific lien placed on one property. The other choices could be placed on several parcels in a subdivision.

547. B. Mortgage warehousing involves borrowing on groups of loans before they are sold to an investor. It usually takes place after the construction loan and before the take out loan is finalized.

548. A. Tax and tax assessment liens take priority over all other liens (recorded or unrecorded).

549. A. A conduit is a metal pipe in which electrical wiring is installed.

550. C. The action by the license would be described as panic selling and is considered a violation of the Real Estate Law.

551. D. In receiving the check from the buyer, the broker is acting as an agent for the buyer. In such a case, the broker must follow the expressed instructions of the buyer (as long as they are legal). The broker also has an agency obligation to the seller (full disclosure) and an obligation to the rules regarding trust funds.

552. B. Cracks in the wall would indicate that the house has settled in that corner.

553. D. The title company will protect the insured against those matters of record found in any of the offices listed in answer choices A, B, or C.

554. D. An accepted offer would take priority over the listing contract, since it is a statement of agreement between buyer and seller.

555. B. The agent must inform the principal of all offers.

556. D. If escrow receives two termite reports, both reports must be submitted to the buyer and seller. Buyer and seller will decide which one to use.

557. C. Lease estates in real property are regarded as personal property, and laws governing personal property apply. Each of the other three items listed is a real property interest.

558. A. The cost of credit reports and appraisal fees are not required to be included in the finance charge.

559. C. 40 acres.

Section 14: 640 acres.

           N 1/2: 320 acres. S 1/2:160 acres. N 1/2: 80 acres. E 1/2: 40 acres.
When doing an area problem if all dimensions are in the same section as in the problem above, just multiply the fractions by themselves and then multiply it times the amount of acres in a section.

$$1/2 \times 12 \times 12 \times 12 = 116 \times 640 = 40$$

560. B. The reasoning behind the answer is that no buyer would pay more for a property than the cost to rebuild the identical type of structure.

561. D. If, after a broker obtained a listing, the seller refused to allow the broker to proceed under the contract; this would be a breach of contract. Because the broker has been damaged, he should sue for damages.

562. D. Loan points were originally created to equalize the return to the lenders on government backed loans with fixed rates where the rates were slow to change, and conventional loans with non-fixed rates which could change daily.

563. D. Under Division 6 of the UCC, the "notice of intent to sell in bulk" is recorded and published to protect the seller, the buyer, and any creditors.

564. A. A Quitclaim Deed delivers whatever interest the grantor may have. As the name implies, the grantor simply "quits" any claim he may have. If he has nothing, the grantee receives nothing. If he has a fee simple title, the deed conveys his fee simple title.

565. A. A minor or incompetent person may receive title to real property without court intervention.

566. B. Under an option the optionee merely has a right to purchase the property. They do not acquire any legal interest in that property until they exercise the option.

567. C. The Government Code requires 180 days notice when the owners are going to convert an apartment to a condominium form of ownership, and the owner/converter, has to give each tenant the opportunity to buy their apartment when the conversion is completed.

568. A. It is legal to split an earned commission with a broker of another state, but such broker must be licensed in the other state (if he or she is not licensed in California).

569. D. The primary purpose of insuring oneself is to replace what is lost, not to lose or gain.

570. C. Severalty means "alone" or "individual." Think of "severed" or "several and separate." A person or corporation can hold title in severalty—that is by one's self or by itself.

571. C. Streets, sewers, etc. are under the direct control of the local authorities (city or county). The Real Estate Commissioner is interested in assuring the buyer in subdivisions under the Department of Real Estate control against fraud. This requires that all commonly owned areas that the developer has promised would be completed are completed. The money to insure the completion of these common areas must be either held in trust or a performance bond be posted.

572. A. Market analysis is a more general term and would include the other choices offered.

573. B. A real estate licensee would be liable for damages to the buyer in the event the licensee acts in excess of the authority given him by the employing client.

574. B. You have to calculate the income based on a $300,000 value and the 6% capitalization rate. Then use the income with the 8% capitalization rate to calculate the new value.

$$I / R = V \text{ or } 6 / 3 = 2$$
$$6 = 2 \times 3 \text{ or } I = V \times R$$
$$I = \$300,000 \times 6\% \ I = \$18,000$$
$$V = I / R \text{ or } V = \$18,000 / 8\%$$
$$V = \$225,000$$

575. D. The Lis Pendens is in effect until the judgment has been rendered and becomes final.

576. A. A Bill of Sale is the receipt that conveys personal property; a Land Contract of Sale is a personal agreement regarding the conditions under which a future transfer of real property may occur; a Chattel Mortgage is an instrument that held personal property as security for a loan, which is later replaced by the use of the security agreement; a Deed conveys real property.

577. B. An executrix is a female person who is named in the decedent's will to administer the estate of the deceased.

578. D. Answer choices A, B, and C refer to people who are specifically exempted by the Real Estate Law from the necessity of maintaining a license. Answer choice D refers to persons known as "Land Locators" and, as such, must maintain a real estate license.

579. D. In most cases, a seller cannot get a deficiency judgment against the buyer if the seller forecloses on a Purchase Money Trust Deed and the sale of the property under the foreclosure does not generate enough to pay off the note. That is, the seller cannot sue for the balance under a Purchase Money Trust Deed.

580. B. A turnkey project is a housing development in which a private contractor has completed the building to the point of readiness for occupancy. The development would then be sold to the customer at a prearranged price.

581. D. The market data approach to appraising is the simplest of the three approaches. It is the easiest to learn and to use. It is the oldest approach.

582. D. The one paying the impounds (the payor) is the only one who can authorize a different expenditure of those funds.

583. B. Front foot values are used to price property but not to show an actual measurement of the land.

584. C. Section 10142 stresses the requirement that a copy of any contract or agreement authorizing a licensee to perform any of the acts for which he is licensed must be given to the person signing it at the time the signature is obtained. If it is given at any other time, the contract may be voided.

585. D. The Real Estate Law stipulates that a salesperson may receive compensation only through his/her employing broker.

586. A. Orientation: Placing a structure on its lot with regard to its exposure to the rays of the sun, prevailing winds, privacy from streets and protection from outside noises.

587. C. An appraisal must be made on the property, but this is not done by FHA. It is referred to as a conditional commitment.

588. D. A homestead may be filed against any of the properties listed in answer choices A, B, or C.

589. D. An ALTA Policy is only issued to institutional lenders. An Extended Coverage Policy of Title Insurance gives essentially the same coverage and is available to private parties, such as the buyer named in the questions.

590. D. A person can homestead only one property at a time. Destroying the home and building does not abandon the homestead.

591. B. This is a definition of Gross National Product (GNP) as used by the federal government.

592. D. There is nothing in agency law or contract law that requires a broker to take a deposit with an offer on real property. The broker should accept the offer and present it to the seller but advise the seller that no deposit was given with the offer.

593. B. In the sale of a business, sales tax is paid on tangible assets, such as trade fixtures and furniture.

594. A. Economic obsolescence results from factors that exist outside the property limits and adversely affect the value of the property. An oversupply of like properties would be such an outside influence.

595. D. A tree that sheds its leaves annually is called a deciduous.

596. B. The real estate law places certain obligations on the broker who is dealing in the loan transactions. If she sells a land contract and collects a commission for her services, she must record the assignment within ten days after close of escrow or after the seller received his funds.

597. B. To obtain a salespersons license one needs to be at least 18 years of age.

598. D. Mechanics liens may be filed within 30 days for subcontractors and within 60 days for general contractors if a notice of completion was filed and within 90 days for either if no notice was filed. Lenders feel it is more important to wait until all lien rights have been passed before releasing the final payment.

599. B. Two implied warranties are that the property has not already been conveyed to anyone else, and that there are no encumbrances against the property other than those revealed by grantor to grantee.

600. C. This is a definition of an attorney-in-fact. Fiduciary refers to a relationship of trust established between people. A principal is one who appoints an agent.

601. D. Siblings are brothers and sisters. They can take title in any of the forms listed. However, they could not take title as community property since that form is limited to husband and wife.

602. D. Section 2079 of the California Civil Code imposes upon the listing broker the duties to visually inspect the property subject of the listing. If, during this visual inspection, any material defect is discovered, the fact of that defect must be disclosed to any and all prospective purchasers.

603. B. When the dominant and servient tenement come under one owner, we have a merger of title, and this terminates the easement.

604. A. Reproduction costs are the most important factor in arriving at a value for fire insurance purposes on a three-year old home.

605. C. Most records relating to real estate brokerage (except those relating to mortgage loan or securities brokerage, which must be kept for four years) must be kept for three years.

606. D. The problem specifically states that the rent is to be $300 per month; therefore, an escalator clause (which would adjust the rent by some index) would least likely be included.

607. C. Generally, the hiring of an apartment or house for an unspecified time is presumed to have been for the length of the time which the parties adopt for the estimation of rent. In the absence of any agreement respecting the length of time of the rent the hiring is presumed to be monthly.

608. C. The deed should not be delivered to the grantee until all conditions of the escrow have been met.

609. A. An estate of inheritance is a fee simple estate, also known as an estate of indefinite duration.

610. B. This covenant or promise, even if not written into the contract, exists in every lease. In the covenant the landlord promises not to disturb the tenant in any way. The landlord cannot be held liable or responsible for noisy neighbors, and the tenant or the landlord may have to take legal action to solve the problem.

611. C. Brokers are urged to remove earned commissions from trust accounts promptly, although they may stay in the account for no more than thirty days.

612. D. Disposition of separate property without a will is: one half to the spouse and one half to one child or, if more than one child, one third to the spouse and two thirds to the children.

613. C. The Civil Rights Act of 1968 grants the authority and responsibility for administering this act to the Department of Housing and Urban Development (HUD).

614. B. It is generally held that the prime reason for a sale and lease-back on the part of the seller is to create working capital.

615. D. To alienate means to transfer or to convey.

616. D. Section 10177 of the Code identifies this illegal activity as "inducement of panic selling" or "blockbusting." Licensees participating in this type of activity could face disciplinary action.

617. C. A Bill of Sale is used to transfer ownership of personal property. Trade fixtures are considered personal property, thus would be transferred by a bill of sale.

618. A. Once a building has been constructed on a given piece of land, it cannot be moved. A developer must use good judgment when selecting a site. A poor selection may lead to a substantial economic loss.

619. B. The loan broker law requires that a true and correct copy of the loan broker statement must be kept on file by the licensee for three years.

620. C. Only easements acquired by prescription can be lost through non-use. Those acquired by deed or reservation in a deed are valid until legally terminated.

621. D. Publicly assisted housing accommodations include all three of these examples, among others.

622. D. The sales tax due on the fixtures must be handled in the manner mentioned in answer choices A, B, and C.

623. A. A homestead exemption protects the claimant against all after-recorded judgments. The fact that the homestead exemption is recorded after action has been started does not affect its position.

624. A. The license should be given to the salesperson; both the broker and the salesperson should notify the Commissioner of the termination.

625. D. FHA and VA loans do not have a prepayment penalty and hard money second trust deeds seldom do. The only loan that would most likely contain a prepayment penalty would be the conventional one.

626. B. The terms: construction loan/interim loan/short term loan all mean the same. The loans usually range from six months to five years in length, with three years being a typical average. Long term loan/take-out loan mean the same.

627. A. Once an offer has been accepted, the deposit belongs to the seller. Agents must follow all lawful instruction of his principal.

628. C. If the agent has no authority from the principal to accept a deposit with an offer, the agent, in that circumstance, accepts such a deposit as the representative of the buyer - even if the agent has an agency agreement with the principal.

629. C. The seller sells the property to the California Department of Veterans Affairs who then sells the property to the veteran under a conditional installment sale contract.

630. C. Analyze the wording in answer choice C. If neither party gave the other five days' notice of termination, the listing would continue indefinitely - a situation not permitted by the California Real Estate Law.

631. A. When in conflict, the most stringent restriction prevails. In this situation, the deed restricts a certain activity, use or building allowance where the zoning laws of the area permit such use, activity or building. Because the deed is considered more stringent, the deed will prevail over the zoning law.

632. C. This action could cause damage to the land to which the water was diverted, by erosion or avulsion. This action would be considered illegal even though Mr. Miller is trying to protect his property by diverting the water to a vacant property.

633. A. Under the regulations of the Veterans Administration, the lender can loan up to 100% of the appraised value. Should the agreed upon purchase price exceed the appraised value, then the veteran has the option of paying the cash difference and still be able to purchase the property.

634. A. The first step should be to analyze the market to determine what the public might be interested in. It would be foolish to develop the land if there is no market for the proposed development.

635. D. All of the answer choices would help to create a tight money market and slow an inflationary trend.

636. B. Transferability is the least important. Utility is the most important.

637. D. The purpose of the "Homestead Act" is to protect the family residence from judgment creditors. If a declarant is not living on the property, it is not his or her residence and thus he or she cannot declare a homestead on it.

638. D. A deed need not be recorded to be considered delivered. As long as it is given to the grantee and accepted, it is considered delivered.

639. B. Acknowledgment is done for recording, which is not necessary to the validity of the deed. A deed may be valid and not be recorded. The deed must have a property description to be valid.

640. D. Adequate financial arrangements must be made for the community, recreational, or for other facilities included in the subdivision offering. The Commissioner is not concerned with the physical aspects of the subdivision, which are regulated by the local authorities under the Map Act.

641. B. The Cal-Vet interest is a "floating" rate.

642. C. The FHA loan program provides that any loss to the government in a foreclosure action is to be made up from the reserve which is built up in the general surplus account of the Mutual Mortgage Insurance Plan. Each borrower is required to pay into this reserve fund. Such borrowers can pay in full at the time the loan is obtained or they can pay the charge over the life of the loan.

643. D. Members of the city and county planning commissions are authorized to make recommendations to the City Council or the County Board of Supervisors regarding subdivisions and zoning laws. They make recommendations, and the City Council or County Board of Supervisors adopts or denies these recommendations. The members of the planning commission are appointed by the City Council or the County Board of Supervisors.

644. B. HUD enforces the Interstate Land Sales Full Disclosure Act.

645. B. It is the obligation of a Real Estate Broker to oversee the activities of his sales force. When he discharges a salesperson for misconduct he must send a statement in writing setting forth the details of the misconduct and the reason for discharge. Under the law, he is required to do this immediately.

646. A. The definition of usury is the conscious charging by a private lender of more than the maximum amount of interest allowed by law.

647. B. The definition of value is the relationship between the thing desired and the potential purchaser.

648. C. Economic obsolescence is caused by outside influences such as zoning laws, inflation, depression, deteriorating neighborhood, or freeway noise. These types of influences are usually impossible to correct.

649. D. All three answer choices A, B, and C are available to Mr. Smith. He may come up with the additional cash as a down payment, re-negotiate the purchase price, or cancel the contract since it was contingent upon the ability to obtain a loan for the full purchase price.

650. D. Since the deed was not delivered and was fraudulently recorded, title did not pass and remains vested in Jones, the grantor.

651. D. An Abstract of Title is a summary of conveyances and other facts that relate to the property's title. The Policy of Title Insurance insures that the property owner will not suffer the loss if the title is imperfect.

652. B. The definition of "company dollar" is the income of an office after all commissions have been subtracted.

653. D. Advance fees must be deposited into a trust account and disbursed only to pay advertising expenditures used for the property that is the subject of the listing agreement.

654. D. Since Allen left an invalid will and has no heirs, the property will escheat to the state subject to the existing lease.

655. D. The client's proposed use of the property determines the appraiser's approach.

656. B. The CRV is the Federal Veterans Administration appraisal commitment of property value, and is required under federal law on all VA purchases.

657. B. The definition of a customer is a prospective buyer in a listing.

658. A. The seller of real estate property containing one to four residential units must provide the buyer with a transfer disclosure statement.

659. D. The Law of Agency requires an agent to disclose all facts concerning a transaction to his principal. Violation of this agency relationship makes the broker liable for disciplinary action by the Commissioner, as well as for a civil suit by the principal for recovery of undisclosed profits.

660. C. The holder of a life estate has rights in the property only as long as the designated life exists. Upon the death of Mrs. Fields, her rights ended.

661. A. A percentage lease is based on the gross income of the tenant and provides for a minimum guaranteed rent. Since the tenant only pays a minimum amount each month until the business increases, it also aids the landlord in that the rental income will increase as the tenant's business increases.

662. C. Wear and tear is a form of physical deterioration and not a form of obsolescence.

663. C. Conditions and contingencies should be as complete as soon as possible and show a time limitation. With the 20-day stipulation, the seller will be released from her obligation and will have the option to extend or grant additional time to the buyer, or to find another buyer.

664. A. Income tax liens are classified as general liens.

665. B. A listing agreement is merely an employment contract where the owners hire the agent to represent them in dealing with third parties. Since it is a contract, it requires a "meeting of the minds."

666. A. When calculating the square footage of a home, you must consider the house and garage and you measure from the outside area.

667. B. A sublease transfers possession of property from the lessor to the lessee. A mortgage and a security agreement are used in borrowing money, and an easement gives the right to use someone else's property. With an easement, that right to use is usually not an exclusive right to use or a right to possess.

668. D. The extension continues from period to period and would be known as a month-to-month tenancy.

669. A. The assessed value for the property has nothing to do with its market value and would not be considered by the appraiser.

670. D. An estate for years must be for a designated period as given in the question; this is personal property because it is temporary. It is also known as a Chattel Real, and is a less- than-freehold estate.

671. C. The Department of Fair Employment and Housing enforces fair housing laws on the state level. Complaints must be filed within 60 days.

672. D. The injured party may select any of the three remedies listed.

673. B. The definition of a hip roof is a roof with four sloping sides rising to the ridge board.

674. D. In a Trust Deed transaction the trustee receives the "bare legal title" but no possessory interest. He merely holds the title in trust.

675. B. Under RESPA, finder's fees are illegal and would never be found on the Uniform Settlement Statement.

676. D. Since Coconut is still alive, the estate will remain in Banana's family and will go to his heirs until Coconut's death.

677. A. Since the deposit was 1%, the amount is $400. The seller collected the $400, but had agreed to pay one-half of that amounts to the broker in the event of the buyer's default.

678. A. If the grantor sells "subject to" the loan, the grantor keeps all of the liability. In the other three choices, the grantee has no liability.

679. D. Constructive eviction occurs when the tenant's use of the premises is substantially disturbed by the landlord's actions or his failure to act where there is a duty to act.

680. D. "Severalty" means "individual" or "alone."

681. B. If a person owns property in California, he may sell that property while he is in another state. The deed could be drawn and acknowledged out of state.

682. D. When a trustee forecloses, they record a notice of default and wait three months to see if the borrower can reinstate the loan. If the borrower does not, they proceed with the Notice of Sale.

683. B. The seller becomes the new lessee and all future rent paid to the buyer is a deductible expense for the seller for income tax purposes. The transaction does not defer any capital gain.

684. C. Stock in a mutual water company is real property. It is a corporation created to provide water for designated parcels, the owners of which own stocks in that corporation. The law requires that the stocks be passed to the new owner upon the sale of one of these parcels.

685. A. The section due west of section 18 is actually in the next township to the west. This would be section 13.

686. C. The Statute of Frauds is the California law that spells out which contracts must be in writing in order to be enforceable in court. Commission splits are not included.

687. A. Even though the well and pump are put in the ground, the tax assessor classifies these as improvements.

688. A. This relieves the seller of the primary liability. Taking title subject to the Trust Deed and note leaves the liability in the seller's hands.

689. D. A land project is a special type of California subdivision in which the buyer has a 14-day rescission period.

690. D. The main purpose of RESPA is to provide consumers with enough information to shop for settlement services.

691. A. State sales tax is charged on the portion of the selling price of a retail business that represents value of the furniture and fixtures sold. There is no tax on the value of the goodwill or inventory that will alter be sold at retail.

692. C. According to Article 5, any time a licensee handles a transaction when a Trust Deed or a land contract is conveyed, he must see that it is recorded within 10 working days.

693. D. Price is what one pays for the property. When the terms are very liberal: low down payment, large Second Trust Deed taken back by the seller, the price would be higher than for an all cash offer.

694. B. "Highest and best use" generally refers to net return on the investment.

695. C. Local minimum building codes only apply in California if they are more stringent than the Uniform State Codes.

696. C. A license is a personal privilege given to someone to use land, revocable by the person who issues it.

697. B. This covenant or promise, even if not written into the contract, exists in every lease. In the covenant the landlord promises not to disturb the tenant in any way. The landlord cannot be held liable or responsible for noisy neighbors and the tenant or the landlord may have to take legal action to solve the problem.

698. D. The standard listing form has the printed phrase "and to accept a deposit thereon." This could be deleted by a seller, in which event the broker would have no authority to accept a deposit as his agent. If under these circumstances a broker receives an offer from a buyer together with a deposit, he would hold the deposit as the agent of the buyer.

699. C. Because the seller under a land contract retains title to the property, he may use that title as security for a mortgage or trust deed loan, but he must be prepared to give clear title by paying off the loan in full by the time the land contract promises are fulfilled, and the buyer is entitled to receive a proper instrument giving him title.

700. D. The Planning Commission is concerned with zoning and development. The Building Inspector and Building Department are concerned with construction. It is their job to see to it that construction meets minimum building codes.

701. A. The broker is the one who has sold the property of which he has a signed offer that has been accepted by the seller, and the buyer has been notified of the acceptance.

702. D. An investor who is interested in leverage is looking to use someone else's money to purchase the property. If the interest rates are low, this is a good factor but under short term financing there would be large monthly payments or a large balloon payment in a very short period of time. This would not be an advantage.

703. D. A landlord must institute court action called an unlawful detainer action in order to evict a tenant.

704. D. Answer choices A, B and C are all correct statements regarding the Real Estate Settlements Procedure Act.

705. C. Economic rent is the rent that is being charged for similar apartments in that neighborhood. If the tenants are on long-term leases, the appraiser must use the contract rent.

706. C. Loss of value from outside influence is referred to as social or Economic Obsolescence.

707. B. The term "compaction" refers to the soil that has been placed in an earth fill and has been pounded down to make it solid or compacted.

708. D. Whenever a description uses distance and direction, it is a Metes and Bounds description.

709. B. The title company insures only against recorded easements and is not responsible for encroachments under the standard policy. The broker is not required to survey each property he sells. The neighbor must pay taxes on the property before he can acquire title by adverse possession. That leaves one solution only - sue for trespass.

710. B. When the dominant and servient tenement come under one owner, we have a merger of title and this terminates the easement.

711. D. Anyone who pays the fee may obtain a certified copy of any inspection report that has been made by a licensed pest control operator.

712. D. Rent from the property is normally prorated to the close of escrow; that is, the seller is entitled to the rent up until the time of escrow and the buyer is entitled to rent from that date forward. Any rent collected prior to the close of escrow which applies to the use of the property after the close of escrow would be a debit to the seller and a credit to the buyer.

713. C. The Mortgage Loan Disclosure Statement does not give a credit rating on the borrower. There is usually a credit report made but the results are not specified in the statement itself.

714. B. Under a listing contract, a broker is employed as an agent for the seller.

715. C. The Department of Veteran Affairs is the California State Agency that is in charge of operating the CAL-VET Program. Under this program, money is procured through a state approved bond issue. This money is then loaned to qualified California Veterans through The Department of Veterans Affairs. The legal title does not pass to the veteran however, but to the Department of Veterans Affairs. A land contract is then created, which guarantees the property will be deeded when the borrowed money is paid in full.

716. B. The husband or the wife is permitted to sign a contract for the sale of community real property, but the other spouse would have one year in which to void the sale. This makes the sale agreement voidable during that year.